For Susie and Joanne

*To the guys in the Guard thanks for the memories
and the camaraderie*

LIFE IN THE LEGION

Adventures of a Roman Re-enactor

Frederick Stacey

Titus Flavius Statianus

Introduction

I have always been interested in history, how we used to live, what life was like back in the day and what makes us who we are now. Ever since my father took my uncle Arnott who'd come down from Scotland and me to visit the ruins at Caerleon in South Wales, the Roman period became my choice of specialist subject although I am interested in all eras of history. A natural progression was to experience it first hand and join a re-enactment society. For twenty five years I served in the Ermine Street Guard, a society dedicated to research and reconstruction of the Romans in Britain in the first century AD. This is my journey across Europe with the Romans.

1

Caerleon with its Roman barracks, Bath house and legionary museum all held a fascination for me and every spare moment was spent exploring the ruins. The best and most interesting of the ruins was and still is the amphitheatre, situated outside the fortress walls. It was here that I had my first experience of The Ermine Street Guard, a meeting that was to have a major impact on my life. It was a meeting that would see me touring Europe and the UK performing the Guards very popular display routines.

A lot of people asked me how I joined the Guard in the first place. Some even take the mickey about me wearing a 'dress' or leather skirt. One of the remits of the Guard is to educate and one of the things to learn is that the 'dress' is in fact a tunic and is made of wool and not leather, Hollywood has a lot to answer for.

How I came to be a Roman Legionary in a re-enactment society was quite by accident.

I'd heard of the Ermine Street Guard through my interest in the ruins at Caerleon but never in a million years would have thought I could join such a group as much as anyone would believe they could join the circus. Twenty five years in the ranks saw me travel Europe, appear in films and television, school visiting and photo shoots performing with the Guard, not to mention the weekend displays.

Over the years, I saw many changes in the Guard both in the line up of members and to the routines themselves. Although there was hard core of regular members, some guys joined to see if they would enjoy it but either they found the commitment too much or it was just not for them.

I went one sunny Sunday afternoon with my then wife Ronny and my daughter Joanne to see the Guard at the amphitheatre at Caerleon in July of nineteen ninety. The Guard were being filmed for a segment on Caerleon for the children's TV program, Blue Peter.

Filming for Blue Peter in 1990

A couple of members that I spoke to in the display tent mentioned that they accept associate members who can get into displays for free and receive Guard newsletters etc. On Sunday evening I wrote a letter to join the associateship of the Guard, posted it Monday then on the Tuesday evening Chris Haines the Guard's administrator and ever on the look out for new recruits phoned me with an offer I couldn't refuse. Did I want to go to France and Belgium with the Guard for free. All I needed was spending money and the willingness to wear the lorica segmentata - the Roman armour . Within the hour I was on the phone to the hospital where I worked to book the time off needed to go on the trip. Ronny encouraged me to go (maybe the thought of a week with me out of the way was tempting). The trip was to take place in September, we would travel by coach from the Guard HQ in Witcombe near Gloucester to Dover for the ferry to Calais. We then made our way across country to the French /Belgian border. Rumour had it that we would be staying in a château.

Poster for Belgian displays

When we arrived at a lovely looking château that had a 13th century barn nearby, it is needless to say we were billeted in the barn that hadn't been used since the 13th century. To get to the bit we were to sleep in, we had to climb a ladder. The toilet was a hole in the ground and to flush it you threw a bucket of water down the hole. It didn't work. As you can imagine with forty plus people using this facility it soon became quite a problem. Another detail was that the water to flush the hole had to be collected from a culvert in the yard. No fun in the middle of the night. So now we come to the sleeping arrangements, as I said earlier this was a barn that hadn't seen use for very many years. There was plenty of floor space so finding a spot away from the snoring fraternity wasn't a problem. The floor was covered in a fine, flour like dust so you couldn't make sudden movements without clouds of white powder filling the air. The windows weren't glazed so at night it became quite cool in there. I'm just trying to give a picture of the kind of accommodation that at times we had to put up with in the Guard. Sometimes it was rough and ready, other times it could be almost be five star luxury.

The Chateau in Belgium

During the night somebody obviously en route to the hole, stumbled and landed on my head. Next morning after having had a fairly goodnights sleep, I sat up to find every space was taken. I looked at the guy next to me and said "Morning" to which came back the reply "Bonjour". During the night we'd been invaded by Belgians, Frenchmen and the Dutch group The Gemina Project.

We were told our wash facilities were "just in the field next door". The field next door was in fact a mile away in a kind of caravan, across a muddy bog, an electric fence, a road and hill into the field. Thankfully the electric fence was turned off while the entire Guard clambered over it. As we made our way up the hill, Roy Green (name changed to protect the guilty of which you will hear more of him later) had forgotten his towel so had to trek back down the hill and over the electric fence, which by this time had been turned back on. It certainly made his toes curl not to mention his nether regions. The entire guard took the mickey out of him for the rest of the day. Roy Green was a strange character described by one member as 'an evolutionary cul-de-sac' which I thought was a fairly accurate description but more about him later. This trip to France and Belgium was my first time out with the Guard so I wasn't sure what to expect.

The morning of our first display we were taken to the display area, which appeared to be in the middle of nowhere. There were a few mutterings in the ranks that we probably wouldn't get many people to come and see us. The organisers assured us that because there were a lot of outlying villages, the people always show up for big events. "How many are likely to come" asked Chris Haines. "Oh we expect a few thousand" came the reply. We admired their optimism but thought the estimate a bit on the high side. How wrong we were. The Dutch group The Gemina Project had joined us so they needed some rehearsal with our display routines. I too would benefit from some guidance as it was my first time. I was placed between two experienced members, Andrew Learner and Derek Phipps, who were to give me directions during the rehearsal. Whilst we marched up and down the arena in our civvies, we could see coach after coach pulling into the designated parking area.

For the first display we had the few thousand that was promised, by the second display we had several thousand people watching us. Because it was so new to me I was too busy concentrating on getting it right to notice the crowd. The armour I had been allocated fitted where it touched and the sandals hurt my feet. It's a wonder I stayed with the Guard for so long.

Once we had completed the displays in Belgium it was time to pack up and head for a little town in Northern France called Bavay. Our accommodation was a school dormitory the usual occupants being away for half term.

At first light Chris came around tipping selected members from their sleeping bags. This, I was to discover would be the routine for nearly every Guard job. After breakfast we went to inspect the arena and erect the display tent and set up the artillery. The arena turned out to be a disused sports field with a wall made from bales of hay for the artillery to aim at.

The field wasn't level and there was a curb partially hidden by grass. This was to cause me much grief. Not being used to the displays or wearing the armour, in particular the sandals, I found I was quite tired. The last display of the day went well to the appreciation of the crowds. Unfortunately being tired I managed to catch my foot on the edge of the curbstone and ploughed head first into the crowd. One thing I should mention was that this took place during the charge. The charge is the highpoint of the display when the entire Guard forms a wedge shape, draws the gladius and as we march slowly towards the crowd we beat our shields. A few feet from the crowd we break into a run and screaming at the top of our voices charge at the audience. It has a tremendous effect and goes down very well with the crowd. It is also the demarcation from the drill part of the display to the shooting of the artillery.

Setting up the artillery, Bavay, France

For a few minutes I didn't know what had happened. All I can remember is looking up and being helped to my feet by a group of Frenchmen.

Before we did the display in Bavay we did a promotional march around the town. This was to prove to be the most arduous part of the trip for me. Boots that didn't fit properly and hard roads and armour that pressed into my shoulders didn't exactly make for a comfortable march, but being the tough nut that I am I persevered and although it was painful on the feet I quite enjoyed it.

We marched around the streets of the town but there wasn't much response. A few people stopped to watch, but the big crowds weren't forthcoming. There were small posters advertising our presence pinned to the odd lamp post but after marching through few more streets we were thinking things were going to be a bit flat.

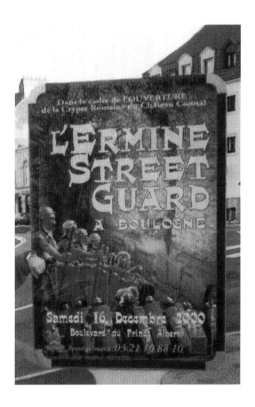

We turned into the town square and couldn't believe our eyes. It was like the liberation of France. People were hanging out of windows and the streets were lined with hundreds of cheering townspeople. The hair on the back of my neck stood up and I thought to myself "I like this"

With the crowd egging us on, we went into hero mode. The marching became better and we stood more to attention than ever. "This is definitely for me" I thought and although I had blisters on my feet, I continued to march like a seasoned pro. I did a one point catch my foot on a protruding rock and almost took a tumble but managed to right myself and carry on.

That was my first taste of life as a Roman Legionary. I enjoyed that trip enormously. I fitted into the Guard like a glove and I knew I'd be with them for some time.

This all happened in the latter part of nineteen ninety, we had a few more events in the UK, Hadrian's Wall and a couple of others including some filming at Caerphilly castle for a welsh TV program. The castle was to double as the fortress in Caerleon and worked quite well in the final program. This was my first taste of filming and for the next twenty plus years the Guard and me would hardly be off the TV screens including taking part in famous TV serials. Then it was the close of season. The Guard holds its annual general meeting in November so it gave me an opportunity to get to know the rest of the guys and to look over the past history of the Guard.

So that was my first season with the Guard, it was just enough to get me hooked. That was in the September and October of Nineteen ninety so I was broken in gently with just couple of small jobs and the foreign trip to whet my appetite.

The next season was to be a bit more involved with a full gamut of jobs from filming to displaying up and down the country from Hadrian's Wall to Caerleon in South Wales.

2

First off in March is the pre-season meeting. This is where the Guard prepares for the year ahead, repairing, cleaning and making new pieces of kit. I had been allocated the kit that I'd used on the France /Belgium trip and it needed repairing (the bronze hooks holding it together have a short lifespan) and it needed cleaning. The lorica wasn't the best fit but after wearing it for a few years it became fairly comfortable. I think that in fact I had just moulded into the shape. Unfortunately in later years middle age spread had added a few pounds and the armour didn't fit so well again.

The nineteen ninety-one season had the usual run of jobs including my "home" territory of Caerleon. When I first joined the Guard we did three displays a day and Caerleon was an annual event but later the displays were cut to two a day and our appearances there bi-annual. Because we did Caerleon in my second year my wife and daughter came to see me performing with the Guard. I'm not sure what my daughter Joanne made of it seeing "daddy" dressed up in a suit of armour and charging at the crowd but I have a slight inkling of what she did think from her watching a TV program, which featured the Guard, the program we filmed in Caerphilly castle. The program was made by HTV Wales and featured historical scenarios. It was called Day Return and featured a blue double decker bus. On board were four people who arrived at various locations and strangely enough were transported back in time and they then became the characters from that period. In our case it was a few Celts and Caradoc. The Guard was featured in two episodes. As I said earlier some of the filming was done at Caerphilly castle and also Cosmeston Celtic village near Barry and Dyffryn Gardens just outside Cardiff. At the Celtic village the

Guard - the approaching Romans had to raid the village tipping over tables and generally searching. One scene involved a small lad who wanted to be a warrior holding up a sword to the Romans in defiance. A Roman soldier (not a member of the Guard but an actor, because he had to laugh loudly – it was considered "acting") approached the lad and cracked his head open with his gladius. It was quite graphic for the kind of program but there we go. When it was shown on TV it had the seven o'clock spot on a Tuesday evening. I was working so I got Ronny to record it so I could watch it when I got home. Because I was in it somewhere, Ronny and Joanne watched it. Joanne, who was about four years old watched as the actor smashed the sword on the young boys head. You never actually saw the sword make contact but it was obvious what had taken place. The next shot showed the lad obviously dead, lying on the ground with a trickle of blood on his face.

Daddy's girl

The upshot was that when Joanne was asked in school a couple of days later "What does your Daddy do?" her reply caused a little concern to the teachers. "My Daddy waves a sword around and hits boys on the head until blood comes out." The next visit to the school we were greeted with "Ah, Mr. and Mrs. Stacey, might I have a word?" After explaining and satisfying the teachers that I wasn't a child killer, (twenty three years later I played that part in a National Geographic documentary featuring the Guard), they persuaded me to visit the school in kit and "Talk about the Romans". I was to visit the school on many occasions in the following years.

Ronny, Jo and founding Guard member Bill Mayes

In that year we had the usual foreign trip which was to be a return visit for the Guard to a town called Martigny in Switzerland. I had always wanted to visit Switzerland and this was the perfect opportunity. We arrived at the Guard HQ on the night before we were to travel to load the truck. Then in the early morning we set off for Dover and the ferry. The coach company that the Guard had hired got us as far as France and on a steep incline the bus overheated which meant us stopping half way up a hill for an hour while the engine cooled down. The hill wasn't very steep more of a long incline which gives you a fair indication of the state of the vehicle. While we waited by the roadside some of the lads wandered into the long grass myself included. Here we came across some of the local wildlife. Praying mantis and yellow and black spiders, which weren't exactly tiny. It didn't take me long to tuck the bottoms of my trousers in. The thing about spiders is they go from nought to sixty in two seconds flat, without warning. It's a shame our coach didn't have the same ability.

Waiting for the coach to cool

Once the drivers of the coach decided that the engine
was cool enough we continued onward and upward so to speak, at the leisurely pace of about ten to twenty miles an hour. Eventually we arrived in the little town of Martigny. Our accommodation was in a former convent that was used as a hostel or something similar.

The former convent in Martigny

The Guard having been on the road for twenty or so hours needed a shower and something to eat. A little local restaurant was procured for the Guards' use and we were told what rations we were allowed. This was where we were to have breakfast as well. We were in Martigny to give displays as part of the opening ceremony of the newly refurbished amphitheatre. The Guard unloaded the kit and did some running repairs before a rehearsal. The arena had the previous few nights played host to an orchestra, but when we marched into the arena we discovered the centre was ankle deep in water. Great! What an interesting display this was going to be! We did the rehearsal managing to avoid the minor lake in the centre. When we did our first display for the local dignitaries and guests including some military personnel, the arena had miraculously dried out.

The amphitheatre at Martigny (water in situ)

We had some free time (a rarity on Guard jobs) so a trip to the Grand St. Bernard Pass was arranged. Our not so fantastic coach and our not so co-operative drivers agreed to take some of the lads up there, myself and a few others stayed behind to explore the local area. Apparently it was interesting to see British coach drivers negotiating small winding mountain roads. Scary for the guys in the back.

In Martigny the weather was quite warm, enough for shorts and t-shirts to be worn. Unfortunately the Grand St. Bernard Pass was covered with snow so the lads got some great looks from all the people in their ski wear. Once they all got cold enough it was decided it was time to make their way back down to Martigny. The journey back took them through a small section of Italy, there was a problem as a couple of the lads had not taken their passport so when the border guards went aboard the coach a couple of passports did a second journey to the front.

Top, Running repairs
Bottom, The pained look of armour polishing

Eventually we did our displays to an appreciative audience in the amphitheatre then it was time for the journey home. This proved to be a feat and a half. The coach wasn't up to long distance travel and the drivers weren't keen on us using the facilities. The Guard being the Guard used them anyway so eventually the toilet unit became full. The fumes from the toilet started to become unbearable inside the coach so the coach drivers were persuaded to stop and unblock it. The weather was quite warm so you can imagine what it was like. We pulled into a service station car park and one of the drivers went outside. There was a bit of thumping and bumping from underneath the bus and the driver climbed aboard and started on his way out of the service station. He had left a pile of human waste in the car park!

The journey took a very long twenty two hours it was very warm, smelly and boy, were we glad to be home. Chris had managed to persuade the drivers to take the coach up Dog Lane, which is at the bottom of the drive to HQ. If you saw this lane you'd think it an impossible feat to get even the smallest lorry or bus along this road but it was done. A few branches on the trees scraped along the bus but everything was fine. After the twenty two hours of uncomfortable travel, all the gear had to be unloaded and some of the lads had to travel back to their homes some a couple of hundred miles away, ready for work the next day. Who said the Romans had it easy.

While I was in Switzerland, immediately after one of the displays, Chris who was never one to miss a sales opportunity got me to set up a sales pitch at the entrance to catch the flow of people entering and leaving the display area. While there I wasn't catching many people although I did make a few sales. Suddenly, almost out of nowhere, came a coach load of Brazilian tourists with more women than men. They made a bee line straight for me and wanted to have their photographs taken with me which involved me having to kiss these shapely and very attractive latina women - oh the hardship! The rest of the Guard were quite envious and a few were suddenly interested in 'helping' me on my stall.

So ended the nineteen ninety two season and with new members joining the society I was already becoming a veteran.

I originally intended to make this "memoir" a chronological account of my time in the Guard, but with so many venues and so many of them revisited, events sometimes blend in to one so from this point it will be only loosely chronological if at all!

3

Nineteen ninety three saw us doing displays in the UK and a mini tour of the French Riviera which was one of my favourite foreign trips during my time in the Guard. Maybe it was because I was younger and there was a core of regular members, so we were more "up for it" so to speak.

We flew into Toulouse airport and picked up a coach that was to take us to our accommodation, the usual schools and sports halls. As you can imagine, the weather on the French Riviera was rather warm, so it would be "uncomfortable" to say the least when doing the displays. The one thing I found on this trip was that if I was offered a drink then I would take it (as long as it wasn't alcohol) even if I only had a sip. I found throughout the trip that I was fine. Whereas others took the wine when it was offered and they seemed to suffer a lot. Save the booze for the evenings when it was cooler and you'll be OK. Morality tale over, back to the memoirs...... We did the usual promotional marches around the towns and for the French, mad dogs and Englishmen (and Welsh and Scots) really do go out in the midday sun!

Newspaper clipping from Perpignan

These jaunts around town were short promos to spark a bit of interest in our displays. They had the desired effect as our displays were always very well attended. One display was on the top of a hill overlooking the town and was to take place at night under floodlighting. We went and had a look at the site and have a quick rehearsal and found that the ground was covered with dry bracken which was a bit harsh on the legs. Also we were pulling bits of pottery out the ground. Time for some fun. Chris had a large amphorae made for our static camp displays. It had cost a lot of money and was carried in a specially constructed padded box. He was quite precious about it and you felt his wrath if you didn't treat the box and it's contents with respect. Whilst we were setting up ready for the show in the "parade/display" area, I found a piece of amphorae handle that matched perfectly the one on the reconstructed amphorae. Whilst nobody was looking

I smuggled it into the box. I called a couple of the lads over and told them to watch Chris's face. I opened the lid of the box and shouted "Oh dear" or words to that effect whilst feigning shock, when Chris looked over he started to shout "What's wrong?" At that point I lifted the "broken" handle out of the box. His face was a picture as his temper started to unleash. He went on a diatribe about not being careful when handling gear. Of course when he reached the box the amphorae was intact. Thankfully he saw the funny side (eventually).

It was quite a strange event as we don't normally display at night under floodlights also they had constructed a grandstand for the audience, we hoped that they thought we were worth it!

As we marched up and down creating clouds of dust and destroying the archaeology, the sound technician was running a sound check. In the UK when people test sound systems they tend to say "one, one, two" into the microphone. In France they do the same thing except one two is replaced with the French equivalent – "Un, un deux". As we marched up and down, across the sound system came the sound of someone apparently having sex. "Uhn, uhn uuun deux, which with the Guards' sense of humour the giggles soon set in.

When we did the displays it was to a capacity crowd and went down extremely well. Our armour looked good under the floodlighting which was just as well considering the state of some of the kit. Once the show was over however, we started to pack away our stuff when suddenly they killed the floodlights. In absolute darkness we switched on the range rovers' headlights which gave some light but not nearly enough. Once everything was packed on the truck, we set off for the next venue. Unfortunately at the next venue we discovered we'd left two metal chairs behind. When the archaeologists start to examine that site they will discover that the Romans had folding metal chairs just like in the twenty-first century!

We did displays at various venues along the Riviera including Perpignan, Narbonne and others. In Narbonne, Chris gave out our (the newish members, those who'd been in for a year or so)

Roman names. These were researched by someone in the British Museum to closely match our jobs or lifestyle, mine is Titus Flavius Statianus a bit of a mouthful and always raises a titter or two, I usually abbreviate it to Tit. Flav. Stat. which causes more giggles. The interesting thing about it is that the name comes from a real person who actually existed. Not only that, the person existed in Narbonne so I was reborn on the French Riviera in Narbonne. Titus Flavius Statianus was a Gaul who worked with Greek pathologists / medics which sort of matches my day job. I work in the health service and at the time of my naming I was a pathology assistant. I've since moved into endoscopy and from there went on to train and qualify as a Clinical Technologist in Nuclear Medicine.

We were given real/realistic Roman names for the purposes of children who would be asking the soldiers for autographs. Signing "Best Wishes, Fred Stacey" would be met with strange looks and would go down like the proverbial lead balloon.

At a town called Laudan we were guests of the French Foreign Legion and were shown into this office to meet with a commander. As we made our way across to the office we mentioned to Chris that he shouldn't accept any coins, just in case we ended up wearing a kepi and were posted off to some distant outpost. Never really saw myself as Beau Geste. We were in fact to be *presented* with a kepi (the legionaires hat) not only that it was a white kepi which is only given to legionaires who have "passed out". We were also presented with a Colonels' rank tabs and a cast bronze medallion. These are at the headquarters in Gloucestershire but are not as yet on display.

Sports hall accommodation, South of France.

We had some free time on this trip so we headed for the beach. Unfortunately it was not the fancy playground of the rich beach that you see in the brochures, but we are the Guard and roughing it is part and parcel of being a member. It wasn't that bad but the beaches were just the same as back home – except the sun was out and the water clearer!

The French Riviera trip is one that stands out to me as the membership of the Guard was the original line up that I joined.

Foreign trips were a highlight of my Guard membership and I seemed to have acquired the nickname "Foreign trip Freddie", in fact I missed a couple of jobs one year and when I showed up for the next job the guys were saying "Why are you here, we're not going abroad!" - Touche!

4

Back in the UK and back to earth, we had the usual round of jobs including a trip to Hadrian's Wall. The Wall is a special place for the Guard as it has close links with the sites, in particular Vindolanda. They also have a tradition in the Guard that at least one day is set aside for a wall walk, visiting some of the sites. The problem when doing displays was you didn't get to have a proper look at the remains. As the Wall was a long haul for many members, we tried to build in an extra day for us to have either a museum visit or a walk along the wall visiting remains.

Hadrian's Wall walk

Aside from the main jobs members are also asked to do school visits and other jobs that require just a few or even one person. For a time I was the only member in the South Wales area and I lived about a mile and a half from the museum at Caerleon so whenever they needed a Roman soldier it was me who was asked. A local newspaper did a "This is your life" type article where they ask members of the local community a series of questions about their lives. I was asked to meet the journalist and photographer at the museum. I arrived and duly put on my armour and went outside to speak to the journalist. All was going well with the photographer clicking away asking for this and that pose (which ever that one is). A "real" Roman soldier outside the museum caused a bit of stir with tourists and I was immediately mobbed by a couple of Americans asking if they could have a picture. I'm always one for international relations although I draw the line at the "special relationship" so I couldn't say no to them standing next to me and having a picture. The photographer was getting more and more exasperated until in the end he exploded and started yelling "We're trying to do a photo shoot here,why don't you piss off". The yanks weren't impressed and went off muttering something. "Otis let's get away from this nasty Brit". The photo shoot went well after that and the finished article was OK even if I did seem a bit of a dick in some of it. Most people said I came across as a "nice bloke".

Lifed by the South Wales Argus

Over the years I have been to various openings at the museum, when the Capricorn Centre - the reconstructed barrack room and education centre was opened they had the ex Blue Peter presenter and actor Tim Vincent there, with me as the token Roman soldier. It was good to have a well known face opening the new department. It was good of Tim Vincent to be there as well.......

One time at the last minute Chris asked if I would be the token soldier again to the opening of the Pegasus Centre which is an extension of the education centre. I had to rush to the museum after work and my kit was in a bit of a state but I managed to clean some of it. There were no famous celebrities (apart from me, of course!) to officiate this time as it was being opened by the Mayor of Newport. On the photo that appeared in the paper I looked as if I'd been dragged through a hedge. My tunic looked as if I'd slept in it and got it caught in a door. Thank god it was yesterday's news.

When I first joined the Guard I was working in a hospital as a porter and was working a rotating shift pattern that included nights. In nineteen ninety one I was in the land of nod after a night shift when the phone rang. On the other end a voice said something like "This is Ruth Prince from BBC Radio Wales, I wonder if you could come to the studio and talk about the Celtica Festivities" Having just woken up with a start, I was bewildered as to why the BBC were calling me and not knowing where I was I explained that I was working nights and could she call later. I didn't even know the event was called Celtica Festival further adding to my confusion. When she did call later she asked loads of questions about the Guard, the Romans and Caerleon. I enthusiastically answered each question at length thinking she was genuinely interested in what I had to say. I was so naive in those days, (what do you mean nothings changed). They wanted me to wear my kit into broadcasting house in Llandaff, Cardiff. Only thing was it was for a radio programme and the presenter wasn't even there, he was in a studio in Swansea. I didn't wear the kit as I would have caused some accidents on the roads outside the BBC. When I'd got there I was sat in the foyer amongst a plethora of thespians waiting for auditions and their CTPO (cue to piss off). I was shown into a studio and sat at a desk, some headphones were plonked on my head whilst the producer disappeared out the door and was looking at me from behind a pane of glass. Now I know how the monkeys feel at the zoo! A voice appeared in my headphones from a man who was somewhere in Wales. "Hello Fred" came the voice. "Uh hiya" I said nervously. I didn't have any media experience and it showed. The man - Mal Pope asked me all the same questions that the producer asked me. Unfortunately, he didn't have the same "interested" manner of the producer and his questioning bordered on taking the mickey. My answers were stilted and didn't come across well. I think if the presenter had asked the questions first instead of the producer using me for research first, I probably would have answered with the same enthusiasm that I had when the producer first called. She should have recorded our telephone conversation! Since then I've been on a radio presentation course and at the time of writing, have a radio show of my own. Still, they sent me a cheque for nineteen quid for expenses which was unexpected and I have the interview on cassette for posterity. I'll have to digitise it one day, once I find it again.

These small time jobs were often quite enjoyable and could be a bit of a laugh when your with a few of the lads. But there are times when you'd rather be anywhere than in kit. Every year, a few members of the Guard turn out for the annual Caerleon Birthday Lectures which takes place every September the twenty third. This date is the birthday of the founding of the Second Augustan Legion, the unit who were based at Caerleon. The lecture takes the form of the Guard parading the standards of the legion, a lecture on a subject relating to Roman archaeology and, back at the museum a toast to the legion (canapes and hooch).

Parading the Standards at Caerleon

The Guard in my early days of membership, performed at Caerleon every year and for three times a day over a weekend. Every year I seemed to get collared by a man clad in motorcycle leathers with an earing in his ear - a bohemian character. He'd ask me lots of questions about the Romans and the occupation of Caerleon to which I would answer to the best of my knowledge. One evening at the birthday lectures we, the Guard fulfilled our role to parade the standards. We took our seats which were right at the front and settled down as Richard Brewer of the National Museums and Galleries of Wales, gave an introductory speech and announced the guest speaker for the lecture, Professor Mike Jarrett - Archaeologist. The lecturer stood up and took to the podium. I looked up and as I was clapping along with everyone else started to slink deep into my seat. It was the man in leather who kept asking me awkward questions about the Romans. I should have in hindsight joined him on the podium and asked him some awkward questions! I didn't see him at any more displays after that and later found out that he had in fact died.

Another time Chris asked if I would be the token Roman at Swansea museum. I'd been there before with Chris and someone else and Chris thought it a waste of time and because he'd travelled from Gloucestershire decided that it was too long a journey for such a boring day. I must admit the visitor numbers were rather on the low side. Anyway, I'd agreed for the second time to be the token Roman for a day in the museum. They asked if I could stand upstairs and just speak to people and answer questions about the Romans as and when they came in. I stood in the gallery for ages before anyone arrived and they just nodded and said hello. Then went on their merry way away from this nutter dressed as a Roman! I was standing by a display case when some youngsters came in and when I said "Hello" they jumped out of their skin. That was it. To relieve the boredom I'd stand absolutely still and when anyone came in I'd wait until they were near me and just suddenly start to move and speak. It certainly relieved the boredom for a time. I was asked back again but strangely enough I was unable to spare the time.

From time to time in this account of my time with the Guard I will go off at a tangent with these little stories as and when I remember them. As I've said earlier, jobs in the Guard tend to blend into one especially as we return to some venues year after year.

Sometimes I think something happened on such and such a trip when if fact it was the one before it or the one after, but essentially they happened at sometime within my tenure as a Roman soldier!

5

At the beginning of this memoire I mentioned a character called Roy Green - the evolutionary cul-de-sac. I seemed to pair up with this character because we were from the same neck of the woods. He was a bit weird in so much that he was into World Wrestling Federation stuff, to me that would probably be a gays paradise and from talking to him he seemed to know a lot about amyl nitrate and frequented a gay club in Cardiff. He wasn't gay, just kinky. As his dossier grew I avoided him more and more until we did a job in Carlisle. In nineteen ninety one The Tully House museum had been refurbished and was to be opened by Her Majesty the Queen and we were to provide a guard of honour. Chris in his infinite wisdom decided that because Roy and I were from South Wales (at that time there was only three and the other one wasn't there) he'd put us to share a hotel room. The room was a twin bedded affair and was comfy with an en suite bathroom. Off we went up the stairs to the room, plonked our things down and sat on our beds. "This is alright, isn't it?" said Roy "It makes a nice change to have a decent billet" I said. Roy sat on his bed and I sat on mine. Then came the bombshell. "How about a bit of mutual masturbation?" he asked. "Fuck off" I politely replied. "OK" he said and no more was said. I got ready to go out for the evening with the rest of the lads as did Roy. I showered with the door locked and when we returned later that evening I slept very tightly wrapped in the bed sheets just in case! Glad to say, nothing happened. I didn't say anything to the other lads as you can imagine the ribbing would have been intolerable. Sometime after this incident, Roy left the Guard, though not because of it. A good while later I told the Guard of the incident and as expected I was ribbed about it and

Roy became known as "our mutual friend".

Anyway we did the Guard of Honour for her Majesty and stood in the drizzle for hours waiting for her to arrive. As part of the entourage William Whitelaw was with them and I thought he looked very ill. The Queen and Prince Philip made their way up to the museum between the two lines of the Guard and stopped to chat to some of the men. The Queen desperate for something to say asked one of our number, Andrew Learner "Does ones armour get heavier when wet?" Either she had no idea of physics and the fact that metal doesn't absorb water or she was being ironic. We'll never know, Prince Philip on the other hand asked Big Dick - Richard Eastwood why we were there. His reply. "To see you Sir". Why on earth you'd invite Roman soldiers to a predominantly Roman museum on Hadrian's Wall is beyond me!

Her Masjesty on her way into the museum

Once her Majesty and party had entered the building she did the opening ceremony and continued on to the cathedral for a service. We had to make our way to the cathedral entrance where we were to perform the Honour Guard as she came out. We arrived at the appointed place to be told by an over zealous policeman that he knew nothing about it and we weren't coming in. Chris had words (I don't know the exact details) with him or somebody and eventually we took up our places along the pathway out. It took ages for her and her party to come out and we were cold and wet through. As she made her way along the path she stopped and looked directly at me and for a moment she was going to come over and speak to me. Then someone distracted her and off she went and that was the end of my audience with Her Majesty the Queen, to say I was gutted would be an understatement. One thing I forgot to mention was that this took place a day after we'd performed a Guard of Honour for The Princess Royal in Dover. She was there to open the short lived Whitecliffs Experience. As you can imagine it was a nightmare logistically getting all the gear and the men from one end of the country to the other. We lined the route into the venue and waited. And waited. And waited. She took hours to arrive and my feet were killing me but at least the sun was shining. Chris marched up and down making sure we were looking our best when suddenly I had a tap on the back of my helmet. I turned to face a young lad stood on the grass bank behind me, who I could imagine was a bit of a cheeky chappy (putting it mildly). "Who's old brush head then?" he asked referring to Chris's horsehair crest. I explained to him all about the Centurion and his role and I was ever so tempted to call Chris over and get the kid to ask him in exactly the same way that he'd asked me. Chris would have had the kid as a trophy on the end of his vine stick! Anyway I digress, Princess Anne duly arrived and walked up the path to the White Cliffs Experience totally ignoring the Romans along the way. When she was about halfway down the path and in the middle of us, Chris decided to do a salute to her. He suddenly shouted "Away and pray to Princess Anne" or something similar to which we shake our pila in the air and shout "Ave!" three times. This caused the security people with her to reach into their jackets ready to draw their weapons as they thought we were about attack Her Royal Highness. Luckily we'd stopped before they could shoot us all!! Once our stint was over we had a look around the 'Experience'. It was OK but nothing to write home about. Then we had to get everything on the coach including armour, shields and pila and make the long journey to Carlisle. So that was our encounter with royalty, the Queen and her daughter. We were to have encounters with other members of the royal household in the coming years and Prince Charles apparently is a Guard fan. During our trip to Sweden we escorted a member of their Royal family to a function, but more on that later.

6

Over my time in the Guard there seems not to have been a year go by when we weren't on the telly in one documentary or another. When I first saw the Guard they were being filmed for the BBC television program Blue Peter, that was in nineteen ninety, the year that I joined. I have already mentioned the filming at Caerphilly Castle that took place within months of me joining. Since then we've done many children's documentaries, mostly for schools programs but also we took part in a children's drama called Aquila. This was about two schoolboys who discover a time capsule in a cave that can go back in time to the Roman occupation. We were in the final part when they discover the true owner of the ship which turns out to be a Centurion. We went early one morning to a farm in Gloucestershire where these scenes were being filmed. It was extremely foggy and we arrived at the top of this field to be met by a production person who pointed us in the right direction. "Keep heading in that direction and you'll see it" they said. As we drove through the gloom a double decker bus (the caterers canteen) started to appear then the rest of the production village. As usual it was hurry up and wait and eventually getting "on set". We had to walk down a steep hill and march back up - nothing new there! We did this several times and once at the top we had to all fall down as if we'd been hit by a force. After several "takes" we could go and get some food, change and be off. As it was the last episode and the end of filming there was a bit of a wrap party with cakes and stuff. In the final program, we feature for a few seconds and are indistinguishable as we are viewed from the time capsule- the Aquila. I must say that I personally liked filming whereas if you asked the other members they'd moan about it, yet there never seemed to be a shortage of takers for film shoots!

One unfortunate thing about filming is that it usually took place in the winter when its freezing cold and wet. Once such time was filming for a documentary for W. H. Smith and Cromwell Films about the Boudiccan rebellion. This took place in January at a place in Hampshire called Butser Ancient Farm Project. The project consists of Celtic roundhouse reconstructions with one large house and a few smaller ones all in a large enclosure so as to recreate a Celtic farm village. As it was in January it was a bit of a mud bath with rain on and off. It was also the coldest I had ever felt in my life. The finished video (it was released on VHS) wasn't too bad. It came with a free book that, if you were into scholarly works was quite interesting. We had to do some scenes inside the largest roundhouse that had a lovely fire burning in the centre. Once inside we all jostled for position to be near the fire. Unfortunately when you had to go back outside you felt the cold all the more!

It was during this filming that we had the chance to properly test some of the battle formations and see how effective they were. For one scene the director wanted us to form the wedge and charge at the Celts. We would be running down a slight hill into the waiting Celts. We had reservations about how safe it would be, but the Celts insisted that it would be OK. The director shouted action and we did the march forward banging our shields until we were ready to charge at them. We connected with them and it was quite a fight, the wedge had done its job of splitting the band of Celts into two separate groups that made it easier to attack them. Once the director shouted cut, we discovered just how effective the wedge had been. Three Celts ended up in hospital, two with a puncture wound and one with concussion. We did warn them.

Once I'd returned home from this filming it literally took me three days and several hot baths to feel warm again, I must have been chilled right to the bone. And still I was the first to volunteer for filming!! I must need my head read. I enjoy filming because I use it as an unofficial film school, I watch what the pro's do and see how I can implement it in my own film making.

When I look back at these jobs and how cold and painful they were I wonder how it was that I stayed in the Guard for so long. From the very first job I had painful feet from the ill fitting caligae, it was very tiring and during some manoeuvres I even fell as I did in France. So why did I do it? That was a question that I was asked frequently. I've already said about how I enjoyed filming, I also got a buzz when performing "live" in front of an audience and interacting with the public after the display. All this together with the bitty jobs and the camaraderie with the other lads made for an interesting spare time pursuit. The Ermine Street Guard has been voted the number one Roman re-enactment group on several occasions and has gained the respect of many other groups including other periods of history. Being a part of this brought a certain kudos when you mentioned that you are a member. When I first joined I was just thirty years old and you think the Guard will go on forever and maybe it will, but as we used to say we are an "ageing society" and without youngsters coming in and with retirements and worse the Guard will pass into history. One of the driving forces of the Guard is Chris Haines, he has the contacts, the determination and grit to keep things moving along. What will happen when he retires. We'll just have to wait and see.

Blimey, that was a bit heavy, time to lighten the mood and continue with my journey through my life in the Guard.

7

As I've already mentioned I was trying to make this a chronological account but that is proving difficult but some events and places stand out from the others.

We used to do a lot of filming for a company called Seventh Arts Productions, they did a lot of programs and segments for the History Channel et al. We'd done some filming with them previously and were less than impressed with the finished result. They said it was creative but we said it was out of focus and just of our feet and waists. Anyway they were in the Netherlands filming and wanted to do some shots with the Guard. We did the Roman bit and they then asked if six of us would continue filming dressed as some other ancient warriors (I can't remember who we were supposed to be). We'd been displaying to the public all day and now we had to go through make up and put on these "costumes". The outfits were from the theatrical costumiers Bermans of London and had been flown over especially. I, along with a couple of others had to have a big bushy beard stuck onto our faces, so you can imagine me with ginger hair and a big black bushy beard I looked a right sight. To compliment this I had to wear a tunic that can only be described as being designed by Mary Quant - mmm sweety. Then to top it off a helmet that had a crest on top that made me look like a smurf with a beard. They looked as if they were from the costumes of Flash Gordon or was it Flesh Gordon? Anyway, you get the idea of what we must have looked like and then we had to march across the Syrian desert. Well not really, it was in fact a twelve foot strip of sand at the back of the Archeon - an archaeological theme park in the Netherlands which we'll talk about later. The camera crew had positioned themselves facing towards the sun so that when we marched towards the camera, it put us in semi silhouette (Seventh Arts creativity again). So we got into our positions - a double file carrying a spear and a shield, I think the shield was in fact our Guard shields (apparently nobody would notice once it was in silhouette). The director shouted action and we started towards the camera. Once we'd passed the camera he shouted cut. So far so good. Next he wanted us to start to run when we got to a certain point, so we decided that when we reached a particular bush we'd break into a trot. This we did but it was not good enough for the crew, they wanted us all to start running together. So we decided that on cue one of us would make a sound (they didn't want English spoken on the soundtrack) and then we'd break into a run. The director once again called action and we started to march toward the camera. When we reached the cue point, CJ made the required sound which caused everybody, including the crew to fall about laughing. The sound he made was "Ugg!" Once we'd composed ourselves we had to do it again and again because the "Ugg!" caused us to start giggling like schoolboys. The director Phil Grabsky was starting to get exasperated because the sun was getting quite low so we only had a limited time before it disappeared below the horizon. Eventually we managed to get it right and we were able to go and get the ridiculous outfits off. One of the things I didn't mention was a characteristic of the helmet. I told you about it looking like something from Flash Gordon, but the front also had a point that when we started to run kept smacking us on the nose so by the end of the shoot we had a nice bruise on the bridge of our noses. I never did see the finished result! We seemed to do a lot for Seventh Arts at that time and most of it seemed to be of the "creative" nature.

One of the film and television worlds favourite places to film is at a reconstructed Roman Fort called the Lunt which is near Coventry in a place called Bagindon. It was invariably wet when we filmed there, which for the film people (in particular, the "creative" element) was a godsend as they then asked us to march through puddles while they filmed our feet.

Filming at The Lunt Fort, Bagindon

I recall one weekend we'd been asked to do some filming for a BBC program. It was one of the rare times that the sun was out. We'd all arrived unpacked the gear, got changed while the crew set up where they wanted to film us. We marched to the starting point and did one or two shots of us marching through the gates (we hadn't done that before........!), then they wanted to do some shots of us drilling (parading, not making holes). Just as the director shouted action directly above us the Red Arrows started their aerial display. So we had to wait for half an hour while the show went on above us. It turned out that there was an air show at Coventry Airport and the highlight was a bunch of Romans in the Lunt (OK, it was the Red Arrows). Once the air show was over we continued with the filming. One scene required a Centurion on horseback and Chris was persuaded to get on the horse in kit and ride toward the camera. Once he was in the saddle the horse decided he was having none of it and bolted towards the granary which houses the museum. All we saw was this horse disappear into the distance with Chris who isn't a confident rider, bouncing about until he reached a large bush which he fell into. He said that was the safer option but we'll defer judgement. He decided that his days as a stunt rider were over so instead an actor wore the kit and rode the horse. The reason Chris was to ride the horse was that the full Centurion kit only fitted Chris (he's quite short) so when the actor took over, the kit was mixed with some Legionary armour to make a fit. Not ideal but that's the film and television world for you. At least there was some authenticity about it, if Hollywood were doing it then the kit would be plastic and knitted mail!

More filming at The Lunt Fort, Bagindon

So that was a little bit about the Guard when they were filming, there will be more to say about that later as since I started with the Guard we've done some filming almost every year for one program or channel including a well known drama.

While I'm on the subject of the Lunt Roman Fort it's worth mentioning that this used to be a Guard display venue but unfortunately we tended to outnumber the audience. We have absolutely no idea why this was but people in that village and its surrounds seemed to have no interest in the Roman heritage of the area. The Guard only go there now if it is being used for filming. We sleep and change in the reconstructed Granary which now houses the museum, and after a trip to the pub which isn't close by, we head to the Chinese take away which is in the opposite direction for food. The proprietor would take your order give you a ticket and say "Leemember numba! No numba, no food." The place was tiny and in a quiet village, so you can imagine when forty or so blokes turn up and ask for practically everything on the menu how it must have been in the kitchen. Their takings must have rocketed every time we turned up!

The queue for the chinese, Bagindon

The Lunt was the last place the Guard had it's annual water fight. This seems to have passed into history now as the members are older (not necessarily wiser) but it used to be a lot of fun. The annual water fight took place towards the end of the season and was a highlight in the Guard calendar. Members would dress up in all manner of military costumes and equipment and some of the water pistols would have done riot police proud. It got to the stage where some members had a large tank on their back and electric pumps to jettison the water from the pistol. I remember one of my earliest water fights was at a little village called Acomb near one of the Hadrian's Wall sites. We'd been building up to it towards the end of the season, with members discussing tactics and what equipment they were going to wear. A discussion even started about where the cheapest and best place was to buy super soakers (a type of water pistol / gun) which was at the now defunct Toys R Us. The big day arrived and we settled ourselves down in the youth hostel that was to be our accommodation for the weekend. I think we were performing at Birdoswald Fort although I'm not entirely sure. The evening drew near and the guys started getting kitted up in their uniforms of varying types. It was quite a bizarre spectacle with Anzacs fighting alongside world war one Tommys who in turn were fighting against Japanese snipers! Anyway, as dusk fell the water fight started in earnest with Mark Maillard letting off some thunder flashes (these are fireworks that have a loud bang, known in the army today as battle simulators) they were to lend an air of authenticity. The fight started and water was spraying in all directions and the battle started to spread over the road and into the field opposite.

Within a few minutes a police panda car drew up and out got a solitary copper. I really don't know what he must have thought when he saw all these "adults" dressed up in weird and wonderful outfits wielding water pistols and water canon. He said something about a resident down the road (about two hundred yards away) complained because the week previously a group of other people were causing rowdy behaviour. He then said that if we didn't pipe down that he would take us to the police station. He was driving a Mini Metro. It would have been interesting to see how he'd manage to take us to the station and how the desk sergeant would react to him turning up with three Jap snipers, then having to go back and collect the Anzacs then back again for the Tommy's and so on and so forth. Needless to say it didn't happen and the water fight for that season was brought to an abrupt end. After our brush with the law, I don't think that the water fight took place at all that season. We had water fights in later seasons, but they were few and far between and usually in places where the Guard were the exclusive occupants such as the Lunt.

We did have an interesting final water fight after a multi period event at a place called Kirby Hall in Northamptonshire. One of our newish members came to the event with an old RAF fire tender – yes, you heard right, a bright red fire tender complete with blue lights, helmets and fireman's suits. We kept it under wraps so as to surprise everyone when we turned up. The water fight was taking place in the performance arena after the displays had finished and the public had gone home. A couple of us went in the fire engine to turn up and hose everyone down. Well that was the intention. The ground where the fire tender was stored was quite muddy so it was slow going to get to the arena. Eventually we arrived with blue lights and sirens and got out in full fireman's gear connected the hose and squirted water over everyone. Quite refreshing after a day re-enacting in the hot sun. there was no way we could top that, so the water fight passed into history.

8

We had an invitation to go to Sweden from a lady called Bodil Victorsson to launch a special exhibition, the Romerska Speglingar. We don't usually appear at places that the Romans didn't get to but the funding was in place and the offer was there. Five of us set off from the farm in the Range Rover with the artillery and the rest of the Guard would fly over. We caught a ferry from Harwich to Santander. Boy, its long way to Harwich, it took an age to get there. Once on the continent we headed North to Denmark and on to Sweden. We were to display in Malmo, which is the biggest city in the South of the country. After an exceptionally tiring and long journey we arrived at Bodil's house. She lived on a non working farm that had lots of outbuildings. One such building was being renovated into an education centre. It was here that we were to be billeted. Bodil and her family were excellent hosts providing some magnificent meals and Bodil herself provided musical entertainment - she's an accomplished pianist and guitarist with a fabulous voice.

Bodil

The guys who had flown over were already there and had made themselves at home. After a good nights sleep we went to look at the museum and have a guided tour of the exhibition. We were to display in front of the museum which was cobbled so was really hard on the feet. The sun was out but it was a bit on the chilly side, after all it was late in the season and Sweden late in the season was bound to be cold. We managed to do the displays and generally had a good time.

Bodil entertaining the troops

One evening we had an invitation to go to a meal courtesy of the Swedish army. They wanted a couple of us in kit to add a touch of the spectacular to their dinner. About ten of us were picked up in a troop transporter and taken to the base. We were given soup and some bread (and not much of it) and waited around for our call. Thankfully I wasn't one of the ones in kit. We were hoodwinked, they just wanted a couple of Romans at the meal to which we weren't actually invited and we weren't very happy, but that's life. The exhibition was opened and would tour the country finishing a year later in Stockholm.

We were invited back to close the exhibition and set off once again on our journey to Scandinavia. We caught the ferry and settled in for the long crossing to Santander. While we were on the ferry there were the usual bars and for the entertainment the Stenna Showgirls were to perform. We being the Guard settled in the bar at the back and watched the show from there. When the showgirls came on stage we realised that we should have been sat in the front, which of course, by this time was full. So we didn't get the full experience shall we say and were determined that we'd commandeer the front row on the return journey.

On the journey over I needed to use the toilet and followed the signs from the bar area down some steps and turned left and left again and into the gents loo did my business and returned to the others in the bar. On the return journey I did the same thing, left the bar down some steps turned left and left again and into the toilets. I was in the cubicle when I heard someone else come in. As I sat contemplating, the footsteps came closer and went into the cubicle to my left. I thought they sounded like a woman's high heels. I looked around at the walls and equipment around me and to my shock realised that I was in the ladies loo. The footsteps in the cubicle tried to lock the door but this was obviously broken because she left that cubicle and went into the one on my right. I was trying to think fast - how would I get out of here before she came out and caught me standing there. I sorted myself out and came out of the cubicle and ran for the door. I opened the door to be greeted by a sea of faces all watching me coming out of the ladies. In my embarrassment I turned left down a corridor only to discover that it was a dead end. I had no alternative but to go back the way I came and past the same sea of faces. By now my own face was scarlet the same colour as my sweatshirt. I got back to the bar and the boys asked what happened to me. I gave them my account and took off my sweatshirt, put on my glasses, ruffled my hair and hoped that nobody would recognise me for the rest of the journey.

But that was on the return journey. This trip we were to parade in Stockholm and to drum up some interest we did the usual marches around the town. We changed one Saturday morning and did a little march with just the odd person to watch. The organiser arranged that we would march in the centre of town. To get there it was going to be a very long march which caused a ripple of dissent in the ranks until the organiser spotted a bus heading into town. She ran and caught the bus at a stop and we all had to run, in kit carrying pila (spear) and shield to get the bus into town. How it must have looked with thirty odd Roman soldiers running to catch a bus - bizarre. But not as bizarre as when we got on the bus, it was full of people heading to do their shopping and going to work. There wasn't many seats free but I managed to get one and sat down next to a middle aged lady who had a very bemused look on her face. As I sat there left arm resting on my shield, right holding the pila I turned and said "Morning" and she replied in better English than me "Morning". She couldn't resist to ask what we were doing, so I told her all the details. It must have made everyone's day on that bus giving them something to talk about for hours if not days or weeks, although when we first got on nobody batted an eyelid, they must see thirty plus Romans catching the bus everyday, "Which way to the battle, mate?", "Can I have a return to the war, please?"

Once off the bus we were met by a police car who was going to drive in front of us as we marched through the town. The one thing about Sweden is that it is a big country with a population of about eight or nine million. The town on a Saturday morning wasn't very busy, so the police outrider was really just for show. As it turned out the public were more interested in shopping than watching thirty odd mad Brits marching through town.

Later we set up for our display near the museum in Stockholm, it was October and quite cold. We would be providing a Guard of honour for Crown Princess Victoria when she came to officially close the exhibition.

We lined up outside the museum and waited for her car to arrive and as usual with these things she wasn't on time. When she finally arrived Chris invited her to inspect the Guard and lead her down the two lines of Legionaries we then escorted her into the museum. A couple of us "volunteered" to officiate at the ceremony that took place which meant we'd have to stand to attention throughout. This we did but the only thing was all the speeches were in Swedish and there were musical interludes by what must have been a famous Swedish opera singer, in all it took over an hour. I kept shifting from foot to foot as my feet were killing me. Eventually it was over and we left the room only to stand to attention again while the Princess again walked down the lines of Romans.

Second line up for Princess Victoria of Sweden

We were staying in a five star hotel on this trip - the Ariadne which was situated out of town. We had to catch the tube train to and from the gig which was entertaining in itself, if we missed the train we'd be very late for the displays.

On one of the days it was extremely cold and we were getting ready for our display when it started to snow. We stood in the cold after the display and the Swedes wrapped in their winter clothes were asking if we were "Kalt?" which I think is Swedish-English for "Cold?". The Guard would never admit that we couldn't handle a slight chill, but all the time we were freezing our nuts off.

Richard Morris educating the Swedish public

The next display it had become so cold and the snow was threatening to come on heavier, so we took the initiative and asked if we could display in an empty warehouse next to the museum. After a bit of discussion the go ahead was given and we set about sweeping the floor and making it ready for an audience who would stand around the edge. We would be displaying in the centre.

When we did the display it was to great appreciation from the audience. We weren't sure if the appreciation was for the display or the fact that we'd brought it indoors!

The Swedish warehouse / indoor arena

As we marched up and down in the warehouse, the marching was snappy and loud on the floorboards. We went outside to do the artillery shooting and as you can imagine - it was cold. Once all the displaying was over we had some time to see the sites. We had a walk in a park that had some quirky Swedish houses and in a paddock some moose or mooses? were getting jiggy with it. Later, we had a visit to the Vasa Museet or Vasa Museum. The Vasa was a medieval sailing ship that sank on it's maiden voyage and was preserved in the waters off Sweden. It was brought to the surface and preserved in a polymer/pressure treatment and put on display in its own museum. It was a fantastic day out!

 We were invited by our hosts to visit the Swedish Royal Armouries early one morning. Our guide was going to meet us there and gain us entry. We arrived long before the guide and Chris wanted to know how we get to the entrance so he spotted an armed guard standing to attention in his sentry box. Chris approached the guard just as we noticed that there was a semi circle around the box – a kind of demarcation point. Chris stepped inside the semi circle and proceeded to question the guard. "Chris" we all shouted "step outside the semi circle". He hadn't noticed it and looking down did as we asked. It turns out that if you step inside the semi circle then the guard has every right to take it as a threat and can shoot you. The guard was laughing so I don't think he would have shot Chris but at least he had a sense of humour!

Over the time we were in Stockholm we had to fend for ourselves in the evenings which, in a five star hotel wasn't cheap. In fact I was still paying for the trip for months after I had returned home. We ate the cheapest meal on the menu which was burger and chips which was something like twelve quid a throw (a lot of money in the mid nineteen nighties) plus drinks on top of that! To go into town to a bar would set you back around five pounds for a pint of beer. Not a cheap place to visit and at that time five quid for a beer was extortionate. One thing was we were all in rooms in pairs, towards the end of the tour the members who were to fly home left and those who were left behind decanted into rooms so that individuals weren't in rooms on their own. When the time came to check out, the reception staff asked about some mini bar purchases that some of the guys had made. We told them that they had gone and we heard nothing more of it. To that end I wish I'd made more of the mini bar! Once all the displays were finished it was just the long trip back home, which took about two days by road. One incident I forgot to mention earlier was our run in with the German traffic police. On our way to catch the ferry to Denmark we were driving in the range rover with a trailer full of artillery up the autobahn which was a two lane affair. We were in the "fast" lane off and on (more on than off) and noticed a sign in the central reservation that had a vehicle with a red trailer on it. We were discussing what it meant when it dawned on us that vehicles with trailers weren't allowed in the fast lane - oops. Too late, at that moment a police car behind us put on his lights and sirens and pulled us off the road. We were already on a tight schedule to catch the ferry so this was one delay we could have done without. The German police didn't speak very good English and we didn't speak any German. Chris told us not to say anything that could antagonise them as it might delay us further. What us? We would never do such a thing. Eventually they determined that we would be given an on the spot fine. We would have to pay in cash which at that time was the Mark. We didn't have anything except English currency so they radioed back to base to get a conversion. Chris by this time was desperate to get going otherwise we would miss the ferry and the next one would be the next day. It took ages for them to find out how many Marks there were to the pound but eventually it was found to be about forty pounds. We paid the officers and they then asked what was on the trailer. Chris, not wanting to have take off the tarpaulin which would have been another delay gave the men a booklet that showed what the Guard does, pointing out the artillery pieces. By now we were in such a hurry that he told the police to keep the book, we said wouldn't it be funny if they thought that we were trying to bribe them. So we went on our way and by the skin of our teeth we made the ferry to Gotenburg. It was quite a trip. We never went back to Sweden although I still have contact with Bodil through the social networking site, Facebook. One other thing that happened in Sweden was that one of our auxiliaries Adrian Cook left his wife in England and married Bodil's sister Gudrun. He now lives in Sweden with her and occasionally they come over to the UK and meet up with the Guard. I keep in touch through Facebook.

9

We once had an invitation from the University to do displays in Glasgow. Myself and my co-driver who I think was Russell set off in one of the vans for the long trip up North that was going to take all day. We shared the driving and by the time we got to Scotland it was my turn. It was a bit like returning home as my mother was from Glasgow and we used to visit my Grandmother on occasions. Despite this I didn't know my way around the city but from what I recall it wasn't too bad. We were to go to the University and meet Professor Laurence Keppie, a well known and respected Roman academic. I drove into the University through the exit and was wondering why I was being flashed and waved at! I must have thought that they were just being friendly. Once parked up we found the Prof. and he took us to the student union and bought us a pint while we waited for Chris and the rest of the crew to arrive. They weren't far behind us and we were then shown our accommodation which I think was a church/community hall. Once settled we went back to the students union. We then did the usual pub thing in the evening. Next morning in the drizzle we set up our display on a sports field.

I don't have a much to do with my cousins/family in Scotland - either they are older than me or we just haven't lived close enough for contact, so there wasn't any "family" present that I was aware of. We did the required displays to an appreciative audience although it could have gone better, the weather probably had something to do with it. When we'd finished a display we stood doing the usual meeting and greeting the public that included students from the University. There were two girls that were showing a particular interest and myself and Fitz seemed to be getting along great with them. That evening the Guard had been invited to an event in the students union and these girls were going to be there. We met them at the do and had a really nice evening. One of the girls from the display - a Canadian called Hedda Breckenridge took a shine to me and when the evening was over she was going to walk back to her digs. I, naturally offered to walk her home (can't be too careful with all these weirdos around). Unfortunately Fitz had the same idea so he came along as gooseberry, it wasn't a long way, just couple of streets. My intention was once I'd seen her home was to walk back to the Guard's billet (What do you mean, yeah. right?), it was true as I was a married man! (If only I could have seen into the future......) Anyway once we'd got to her door I gave her a peck on the cheek and Fitz and I tried to find our way back to the billet. We wondered if Glasgow was the place to be wandering around late on a Saturday night? We found our way back without a problem so we must have been in a respectable area!

I can't remember if we did any more displays on that trip but I do remember being given a guided tour of the Antonine Wall by Professor Laurence Keppie. There isn't a massive amount to see of the Wall mainly ditches but as we walked along the sections that could be seen we noticed that some power cables from a pylon lying on the ground. I think they were down for repair but we avoided them just in case. It would have made a great headline had we been frazzled on the Antonine Wall!

Once we'd returned home we carried on with our day to day lives until I got a phone call from Chris to say that he had received a letter from the University and inside was a letter addressed to me. This made me very curious as to who it was from and what they might want (I'd completely forgotten my Canadian friend). I couldn't wait to get to the next Guard job, neither could the rest of the guys.

I opened the letter. It was from Hedda. I could go and stay with her anytime I wanted, all I had to do was call, she really enjoyed my company and would love to see me again. At the bottom was a PS that she would be there for the next five years!! You can imagine what the rest of the guys were like jibing etc. I on the other hand was thinking of how I could get out of my marriage and go and live in Scotland with a Canadian who would probably take me to Canada with her when her course finished. I think the sports firm Breckenridge is a Canadian firm, maybe she was a heiress? I wasn't really thinking all that (OK, it did cross my mind for a moment), but I was quite flattered as she was quite a smart looking girl. I stayed in Newport and in my marriage which ended a few years later. If only I had known that would happen, such is life. I often wonder what would have happened if I had gone along with it, I certainly wouldn't be writing this memoir!

I was married to Ronny (Veronica) for twelve years and went away with the Guard for most of the main jobs without any complaints. Ronny would ask me if I could get a day or two off work for one thing or another and it would be difficult to get the ones she wanted. Chris would phone to ask if I could do an odd job, say, something at the museum or a school job and I'd have no problem. It was just unfortunate that I could get one but not the other. Guard jobs nearly always took place on bank holidays and other public holidays, which caused a bit of friction at times and I think that with Ronny being ten years older than me she wasn't as tolerant with my Guard commitments.

We did try to patch things up with weekends away and the like but eventually she decided that she wanted to be alone. When I came back from the second Swedish trip she had decorated the back bedroom and all my stuff was moved in there. I lived in the back bedroom for around eight months before she bought me out and I moved into a house of my own. I enjoyed the freedom of living on my own but eventually I got lonely. I joined an online dating agency and after meeting some lovely and weird people, met Sue to who I am now married. Sue is a fan of the Guard as they provided an honour guard at our wedding.

She also helped out at some displays if she could get time off work or didn't have other commitments.

SUE and Fred Stacey, of Llantwit Fardre, married at St Illtyd's Church in Upper Church Village. After posing for photographs with soldiers from the Ermin Street Guard, the couple set off for their honeymoon in Scotland.

Newspaper clipping of our wedding complete with Guard of Honour

10

An archaeological theme park was opened in the Netherlands and the Guard along with the Gemina Project provided a Roman presence at the opening ceremony. The Archeon was a large theme park with areas depicting various eras from Stone age right up to the Victorian age. The park was "out of town" shall we say and it was to provide us with our accommodation. We would be staying in a reconstructed Roman farmhouse. We arrived after a very long journey and once settled we climbed into our bunks. The officers, Chris, Martin and crew decided the Principia - the headquarters would be on the second floor in what a modern house would call the attic. Bad choice, the wind blew through the thatch and they found it draughty and cold. Needless to say they moved the next day. I procured myself a top bunk and sorted my sleeping bag and slipping off my sweaty socks I climbed into bed. We couldn't turn off the lights as the Gemina Project boys hadn't arrived and it would have been pitch black dark when they came. I find it difficult enough to sleep on a Guard job, but with the light on I found it even harder. Suddenly from a bunk below mine and diagonally across came a real nasal snore. Heath Williams had no trouble getting off to sleep and began sending them home. I climbed from my bunk and gave him a little nudge to disturb him into turning over. Seconds later he was facing in my direction and really giving it some. I coughed loud enough to wake him slightly and he stopped for all of two seconds. I'd had enough. I needed drastic measures. The sweaty socks that were at the bottom of my bed were just begging to be used as ammo. I rolled them into a ball and threw them with some force directly at Heath. Just as he was snoring on the in breath, my socks caught him straight in the mouth. He woke up coughing and spluttering and I waited for the rail of abuse. He picked up my socks that he'd spat out and handed them back to me with an apology!

I didn't particularly enjoy this trip, it was wet, cold and extremely tiring. There were the fun things like going to the pub. Now, going to the pub on a Guard job can be easy like walking out of the billet and straight into a bar or pub or it can be a challenge. This place was a challenge. The park had a moat surrounding it and a draw bridge that was raised at six o'clock every evening. Our only way out was to climb a fence, climb around some spikes and then shimmy across a large pipe. Great when your sober but coming back with a few beers inside it was a bit like mission impossible. One guy on the return, I can't remember who it was it could have been Heath (with the mouthful of socks) started to crawl along the pipe and was so inept that he slid around underneath and eventually ended up in the water. As you can imagine the Guard were very full of sympathy. Not. Once back to the billet we settled down to sleep and rest with the lights out! The next day was the opening event with the firing of a canon or something else that went bang. Once the day was over, I was glad to get the kit off and try to warm up.

There was just one shower in one of the buildings and we each had a five minute spot in the warmth of the shower – imagine a long line of semi naked men waiting for a measly shower. I have to say I was so cold and tired that it was probably the best shower I'd ever had in my life! It was so nice that I wished I could have stayed longer but the line of blokes outside made sure that each of us didn't take longer than was allowed.

The evening was to be rounded off with a band and disco in the main building, which was a large glass affair that seemed to move in the wind. A couple of the guys stayed in kit and the whole thing was sponsored by Heineken so lager was in plentiful supply. We were given a ticket and told we could have two beers. The ticket system went by the by once we realised that we could have more just by asking. I was with a few guys on the mezzanine looking over onto the dance floor. Next to me was an unattended TV camera that was feeding the video wall behind the stage, it was trained on the dancefloor. I could see Greig and a couple other guys dancing in kit. I know my way around a TV camera so focussed on Greig (he was easy to spot as he's least six and a half foot) as you can you imagine, the place erupted when they saw themselves in all their giant glory on the big screen. Later, myself and couple of the lads, most of whom have left the Guard grabbed a few bottles of lager and went to continue drinking. We decided to go to the medieval section of the park and went into one of the buildings. It was pitch black in there and the only way to find our way around was by feel. All of a sudden a very bright torch was shone into our faces as a security guard who heard the commotion we were making came to investigate. He pulled out a piece of paper and asked for our names, which we gave and thought "When Chris finds out we will be toast". The guard escorted us from the building and took us through several eras of history eventually stopping in the stone age. He then gestured that we could continue our drinking session there. We thanked him and asked his name eventually finding out that he was called Frank. He left us to it and we carried on until we decided that we'd had enough and would go to bed. We crept in quietly and got into bed and just as I was drifting off to sleep, the lights came on and it was time to get up. I was "hanging" all day as we displayed in the drizzle and needless to say I did not return for the next visit when the Guard was there for the closing ceremony (the theme park closed for the winter). I'm glad I didn't go on that trip as it was worse that time round (or so I was informed). The park was much reduced in size when the Guard returned for the second visit, I don't think it was as popular as it was expected. One of the problems with the park was that it was long way from anywhere.

We could see a town from the park but it was across some wasteland that gave it the appearance of a backdrop from a comic strip such as Judge Dredd. It meant the shimmy across the moat and pipe to get onto the post apocalyptic wasteland and then about a mile or so walk to get to the town. The town was a very strange place as there were houses with lights on and ironing boards set up and TV's displaying the local dross but there appeared to be no people. It was like walking through a town where everybody had simply vanished. Eventually we found a bar that had people in and decided that this would be our base. The Bar Quattro was a great little watering hole in the otherwise deserted town. This became our watering hole for the trip.The Guard as usual brought more life to the proceedings by dancing to some of the local tunes, one in particular had caught our fancy. It could only be described as medieval rock. I don't know what it was called but I actually liked it because it became a sort of theme tune for the trip, Greig managed to get a copy on cassette (remember them?). I don't know if he still has it but as cassette tech has been super-seded by CD and that by MP3 the chances are slim. Greig now works for the BBC so he may have access to an archive if he can re-member the title - you never know. Most likely it sounded better in Holland whilst three sheets to the wind.

The Archeon had potential, in 2011 it was still in existence al-though not in the way it was originally.

I must admit that the Archeon experience had put me off visiting the Netherlands again particularly in a Guard capacity.

There was a kind of interesting highlight on that trip when we were to march in Van Damm square to promote our displays and the parks opening. The Guard and a few characters from the park would do a short display. We did a few of our drill manoeuvres and finished with a charge into the crowd which usually sparks a lot of interest. We did the charge and the crowd parted as we "wedged" our way through them, as we came out the other side on the floor in front of us was a gentleman of the road, three sheets to the wind lying on the floor. His face was a picture as thirty or so Roman soldiers ran at and over him. He either went and bought another bottle of whatever it was he was drinking (more potent than his usual tipple - you can see Roman soldiers and everything!) or he gave up the demon drink forever. Once the mini display was over we had to get back to the theme park and as usual this wasn't thought about before hand. We ended up having to march to a train station and wait for a train. The people waiting for trains must have thought they'd died and were in God's waiting room as cave men, Romans and medieval characters turned up. We had to wait for a train and to relieve the boredom we started tapping a rhythm with our spears to which the cave people joined in as did the medievals. You can imagine what it sounded like with the acoustics of a railway station. Eventually we caught a train and set out on our way back to the Archeon. Just like the bus trip in Sweden this was a bizarre journey in kit. Is it me or did I seem to travel on modern transport in foreign lands dressed as a legionary on a bizarrely regular basis! I can't remember what happened after we left the train, it was either nothing much or it was so painful an experience that I've deleted it from memory! Anyway that was the Archeon - the archaeological theme park that seemed to fizzle out, still existed at the time of writing, but much reduced in scale.

11

Back in the UK and we had the usual run of Guard jobs from the North of England to the South at all the usual Roman sites with a few school visits thrown in for good measure. School visiting is part of the Guard's remit and members who are located near a school usually get asked to go and "talk about the Romans". I was at one time the only Guard member in Wales so when a school wanted a visit it would be me that was asked to do it. Most are relatively easy to do with myself in kit talking about the soldiers life and about the invasion with the boys lapping up the gory details and the girls showing disgust at the foods they ate - in particular, dormice (stuffed). They certainly were stuffed if they were about to be eaten! One school in particular had me back a few years on the trot, St Peter's Primary School in Blaenavon. I changed in the boys toilets at the back of the hall and once all the kids were seated I made my grand entrance to the usual gasps of awe and wonder. I would do the usual spiel and let them try on a few bits and pieces like a mail shirt or a helmet. Once this was done and it was time for me to go I would mention to the teacher that I like to have feedback from the kids as to what they thought of it. I do this because it's entertaining for me and it gives the teacher a subject for the kids handwriting and letter writing lesson. I received loads of letters through the post with pictures drawn by the kids which are always hilarious and some are so good I would like to have them on a T-shirt. I shared a few on Facebook at one time or another which raised a few laughs.

Some of the many kids drawings of me

But the bit that I really like is what they say about what they thought. One girl wrote a lovely letter describing what she saw and then she wrote "the best bit was when you came out of the boy's toilets." Make of that what you will. I still look at the letters and pictures from time to time which are still entertaining. One thing of note is the kids who wrote the letters and drew the pictures are now adults and have kids of their own. I wonder what they'd make of the fact that I still have the incriminating evidence.

I remember visiting a school, can't remember which one or where but it was one of the first school visits that I'd done. I was shown into the staff room and was treated like a visiting celebrity. Because it was my first time I was a little nervous (OK, I was cacking myself). They offered me a cup of tea which I accepted as my throat was dry. I was expecting a mug but instead they'd brought out the best china and I had a cup and saucer. As I took the tea from the teacher my hands were shaking so I when I took a sip the cup was clattering on the saucer. So embarrassing!

Working full time I didn't do many school visits unless it was local and either coincided with my shifts or I could book the time off and only then if they desperately needed me.

These little jobs, visiting schools and museums are little asides to the main Guard jobs and can be with another member or three or they could be me on my own. During the half term break in February the Guard - about five or six members set up camp in the garden at the Roman Legionary Museum in Caerleon for a "Come and meet the Romans" day. It was usually quite a sedate day sitting by the camp fire and chatting to any members of the public who wanders by. After we'd done one of these stints in the museum we went for some reason, I can't remember for what, to the Priory across the road from the museum. I bumped into one of the surgeons from the hospital where I worked and as you can imagine he was surprised, one to see me and two, to be dressed the way I was. It blew him away so much that he invited me to one of his surgical dinners. Unfortunately he wanted me in kit and to chat with the guests about the Romans as they milled about waiting for the food. I did it and felt a bit of a Charlie, although quite a few showed some interest. The meal was good and I managed to sit by a nurse that I knew from the hospital theatres so it wasn't too bad, incidentally she was from the Netherlands. He also had a magician who was to provide the after dinner entertainment. He was superb and as usual everyone was left wondering how on earth he did it. I was left wondering why on earth I did it! He asked me on another occasion if I'd do it again but I declined his very kind offer.

12

A former Guard member, Pete Johnson (PJ) and his wife set up a travel company giving guided tours of historical mainly Roman sites. They would tour sites in the day and have a "Roman feast" in the evening. He would invite five or six Guard members to give a talk - a sort of after dinner entertainment. We'd be fed and have a room in the hotel booked for each of us. It was proving quite popular and we did it several times. Chris wanted someone to get into the female costume so asked me if I could recruit someone locally. I didn't get any takers - probably because of how I worded it. "Would you like to come to a hotel with me and dress up in a Roman lady's costume, you'll get dinner and a room for the night?" After restructuring the comment a theatre assistant Emma said she would do it but would not stay the night (I don't think she trusted me entirely) She did the gig and we called her a taxi to take her home. She must have enjoyed the experience because she did it a couple of times after.

On one occasion we had a few hecklers in the crowd and I was constantly being asked by this woman what I had on underneath my tunic. Being part Scottish and wearing a "skirt" I went "commando" I didn't normally but I felt daring that night. She kept on and on and when the time came for us to leave the room I thought I'd give her and the others a treat, as I marched out I lifted the bottom of my tunic (like the tennis girl poster from the seventies). As you can imagine the place was in uproar but unfortunately for me, my spear got jammed in the door and I couldn't get out. After some help from Chris et al I managed to break free and the women were going crazy. One of the punters was videoing the proceedings so I often wonder if it will turn up on one of the "You've been framed" type programs. Still, that little stunt got us loads of drinks at the bar.

I stopped going native for ages after that and only did so on occasions such as if we were abroad and the weather was warm. It certainly gave one a sense of freedom!

13

Going back to filming we did a piece for a BBC Saturday morning children's cookery program called Eggs and Baker which was presented by the Bucks Fizz singer Cheryl Baker. We never actually met her but the filming was done at the Guard HQ and as usual took place in winter. It was cold but at least we could go inside the farmhouse and have a warm between takes. The story was that two kids a boy and a girl were recruited into the Roman army by us and we'd put them through their paces including cooking over an open fire. As it turned out, they didn't actually cook anything - just mixed some herbs and oil together and ate it with some bread. It wasn't particularly pleasant job and the boy was an irritating oik.

When we were setting up the camp scene the film crew thought it would look great if something was roasting over the fire. Tim decided that he'd remedy this and went into the woods with a rifle. After about a half an hour there was a distant crack of a rifle being fired from the woods. Tim reappeared a few minutes later with something to roast over the fire - a magpie! After de-feathering it was stuck on a stick and placed in position over the camp fire. The crew set up the camera to include the roasting magpie and after several takes the bird was much reduced in size. In fact it was just burnt shell on a stick and did nothing for the scene at all. If the animal rights people had got hold of that information I'm sure we'd have had demonstrators at our next display. People watching that program had no idea that the stick in the bottom left of their screens contained a magpie killed in vain!

The finished segment was aired and wasn't too bad really and it included a scene with much respected veteran and founding

Guard member Bill Mayes, now sadly deceased.

These TV things are always a bit tongue in cheek and you never know if the film people or the presenters of the program are taking the mickey, thinking we live like that all the time. Some groups, not necessarily Roman, do tend to live life in kit and seem to think that they are real incarnations of their characters! We, as a society knew when to let it lie and didn't think of ourselves as Roman soldiers but as people interested in a particular hobby. I myself am interested in the Romans in Britain but I am not into the academia of the subject. I was more of a performer, I enjoyed doing the displays and filming and also the little jobs that put us into the public spotlight. As a bonus the camaraderie that we had with the rest of the Guard was great fun as demonstrated in the annual water fight, now unfortunately as already mentioned, consigned to history.

Another of my favourite foreign trips took us on a tour of Portugal. It was another of those arduous trips where we had to be wined, dined and taken a on tour of the country whilst meeting dignitaries from the government etc. It was my first experience of Portugal and I must say that it was a very enjoyable trip. We were to perform at the site of a Roman circus in the South of the country. Then we'd do some displays in the North of the country in fact we didn't have to do much in the way of displays at all. We were there for about ten days and we did just three or four major displays and a couple of promos.

The middle of nowhere. Portugal

The rest of the tour we did just that – tour. Initially we stayed with the Brigada Fiscal in their barracks and were looked after embarrassingly well. The Brigada Fiscal are Portugal's customs police and they provided us with little gifts of a lighter, a flag with their badge on it and a few other bits and bobs that I can't remember. It was a nice gesture and they looked after us very well for the few days that we stayed with them. They provided us with five course meals, all manner of alcoholic beverages and generally entertained us. We did have pangs of guilt about how well we were being looked after and how little we had to do in return.

Brigada Fiscal hospitality - fresh sardines

To give you an idea of how good the trip was I can't remember much about the actual displays but I can remember loads about our free time of which there was plenty. They gave us guided tours of places that even the public don't get to see such as a library containing ancient books from early medieval manuscripts to books just a few hundred years old.

We had time on a beach that was devoid of any people, just us and the Atlantic ocean. The waves were spectacular and we couldn't resist diving into them and being thrown back onto the beach. We had a great time doing this and when we'd had enough we decided to sunbath on the nice clear beach. Whilst we sat soaking up the rays, somebody noticed some flags flying either side of where we were sat. You've guessed it, we had been diving into the waves on a dangerous part of the water and thinking back I can't believe we did it. It was exhilarating diving into the waves but now I can't help thinking how stupid it was given that we could so easily have been swept away. Such is the foolishness of youth (-ish).

Deserted beach, portugal

We paid a visit to Lisbon and as usual I couldn't decide on a present for Joanne and Ronny so I just enjoyed my time there. One thing that struck me about Lisbon was the number of Africans about the place but I suppose Africa wasn't so far away.

We all bundled into the coach and had a few hours to potter around before we had to take off and head for the next venue. On route to the North of the country we encountered some major grass and forest fires that caused us to divert. The driver of the coach and our tour guide each had their own idea about which way to go and they argued and had a major falling out. Quite entertaining once you'd got over the initial embarrassment. We ended up going miles out of our way to avoid the fires but on the upside we did get to see a bit more of rural Portugal, stopping at bars and a stall by the side of the road selling melons, quite refreshing in the hot climate!

Melon stop, rural Portugal

Eventually we reached our next venue and like I said, I don't remember much about the actual displays. It was a great foreign trip and there was a rumour that we'd be going back the year after or the year after that. Unfortunately this trip never materialised but if it had, I'd have been the first to put my name down.

In those days all foreign trips were totally free apart from spending money. With cut backs and the recession etc. we, in later years had to pay a nominal charge to be guaranteed a place. At twenty-five to forty quid it was still a bargain for great time away with the lads. As you've probably guessed and as I've mentioned before, I liked the foreign trips just as long as we were looked after and the venue was in a warm climate. In twenty five years with the Guard I think I've only had two trips abroad that I can honestly say I didn't enjoy one was the Archeon the other a place in Northern France called Samara.

14

The Ermine Street Guard and other re-enactment groups of every period of history were invited by English Heritage to participate in a multi period event at a mansion in Essex called Audley End. They'd had experimented a few years earlier with a small multi-period event at Battle Abbey near Dover that for them went well, for us it was on a slope in long grass. But that's another story. The Audley End weekend was pleasant and in a lovely setting. My brother and his wife lived in Essex at that time so I told them about us being there and it would give them a chance to see me in kit as they'd not seen me dressed like that before.

We did our stuff to the usual applause and then marched back to our camp and the static display. As I stood on duty talking to the public David and Maureen walked up towards me. "What did you think?" I asked. "We caught the very end" they said. Apparently it was so chaotic getting in and parking they missed the very thing they came to see.

So that was the first multi period event that English Heritage trialled and it was such a success that they went on to create History in Action in Northamptonshire at a ruined mansion called Kirby Hall. This was to be a much bigger event with a lot more groups and tradespeople. It was a warm and sunny weekend (one of hottest since records began – but aren't they all?) and the number of people in the crowd was phenomenal. This gig saw me appear (with others) on the cover of the magazine, Military Illustrated.

The first night all the participants turned up at the "plastic camp" the place where they sleep and change into period gear. Then that evening everybody gathers in the beer tent for a few bevvies before turning in. The beer tent is the most bizarre place on earth. The Guard don't wear their kit when off duty for practical reasons as well as the fact that our weapons are real and being drunk in charge of weapons is a criminal offence. So we wore our Guard off duty attire – Sweatshirts and polo shirts. Most of the other groups on the other hand start their weekend as soon as they leave the house and stay in kit all weekend. The beer tent is packed with people from every period of history from World War One tommys having a beer with a Napoleonic soldier and Roundheads chatting to Medieval maidens. A very bizarre place, it was described by someone as "like being in God's waiting room". You can just imagine all these people been killed in battle and being kept in a holding pen until they can be processed. "Sorry ladies and gentlemen, God has been resting after creating a world, we'll get to you as soon as possible. Please accept our hospitality in the mean time"

The History in Action event had been held yearly with a change of venue within the same county, from Kirby Hall to the very large grounds of another mansion called Kelmarsh Hall. This allowed the event to expand with more re-enactment groups and a larger number of traders. Because of the larger grounds they were able have mock battles with recreated aircraft from World War One and a reconstruction of a medieval town. At the very first Kirby Hall event when the last display of the first day was over everybody marched onto a hill nearby whereupon a battle commenced between every period of history. You had Norman soldiers attacking a British army armoured scout car, civil war soldiers fighting with Romans etc. As our weapons are real we were brought to attention with our shields locked together as characters from another time tried in vain to break our defences. All this time other pockets of history were battling it out and cabbages and other vegetables rained down from the medieval mangonel.

Once the battle was over and we started the march back to camp we overheard one of the medievals ask a compatriot "what's for tea?" to which his friend replied "Nothing. We've shot it all at the

Romans!" which as you can imagine caused a ripple of amusement throughout the Guard.

When the displays are over at these multi-period events the first group off after the final parade stand to the side and salute the Guard as we leave the field. Now if you imagine every period of history after the Romans then you will realise that we had to march past them all which is nice until you realise that we then in turn had stand and return the compliment. It took forever just to get back to camp and after a long day displaying all we wanted to do was to get the kit off. On the very first honour salute as we all stood in line either side of the others marching through the middle, a man wearing nothing but a smile jogged past everyone as if we were interrupting his normal jog. When I said he was starkers I meant it – he was totally bald as well!

One thing about English Heritage is they always wanted a lot for very little, they provided us with a large marquee as accommodation but the rest of the facilities left a lot to be desired. Stand pipes for water were few and far between and the portaloos were always miles from where we were and well used. English Heritage tried an experiment and moved the multi-period event to the National Showgrounds at Stoneleigh in Northamptonshire and true to form our tent was miles from the display area.

During the course of the first time at Stoneleigh (the event was held there twice) a massive thunder and lightning storm happened as we were doing our display. The raindrops were very large but we as always, continued with the display even though there was lightning and thunder directly overhead, the public stayed put so we carried on. During a natural break in the performance, Chris went on the commentator's microphone and said "Ladies and Gentlemen, will please stop taking flash photographs as it is making the men nervous". This lightened the mood and caused a ripple of amusement throughout the crowd. I must admit with the flashes of lightning, the rain and the fact that we were carrying seven foot long metal topped sticks did make us very nervous indeed! I did comment that if we were struck then we'd probably all fuse together. I wondered what the scrap value of the Guard would be!!

As I said earlier the display area was a long way from our changing tent so getting to the display site wore us out before we got there. The sun did make an appearance, it was one of those days that had all seasons in one day – raining one minute gloriously hot and sunny the next. On this occasion we were lucky to have a stand pipe near-ish to our tent so David Hare and myself decided that we'd cool off and freshen up in the cool water. As we were away from the public we stripped and had a shower, a couple of female re-enactors went by but ignored the fine figures displayed before them. We decided that we'd do a streak back to the tent (if it was good enough for the guy at Kirby Hall it was good enough for us!). The Guard were cleaning their kit and the ladies were going about their business. Not one person including the women batted an eyelid as two naked men ran past them.

So that was Stoneleigh, English Heritage did it once more at that site then it moved to Kelmarsh Hall which is also in Northamptonshire. Kelmarsh is a much larger site than the previous venues and over a flatter area with a slight hill that was to be a pain in the final parade.. Our display tent was still a long way from the arena and the salutes still took place. One thing was that in order to get to start of the final parade you had to march up the hill and after displaying all day was extremely tiring. Once we'd all marched past the audience we'd stop at the bottom to salute the other groups who would in turn salute us. It still took forever to finish up for the day and with The English Civil War Society marching at a very slow pace took longer than it needed to. As usual God's waiting room was the oasis we'd all head for in the evening and being a captive audience the prices were a bit higher than normal. For novelty value these multi-period displays were quite entertaining, but my preference was for Roman only jobs that featured the Guard as "stars of the show". In some circles we had been called elitist, which of course we weren't, but we did have a certain standard that had to be maintained. We always liked to make sure that what we displayed was as accurate and as close as possible to current understanding as was practically possible. As was said by our esteemed Centurion "We have researched and re-created to a high standard and always strive for the best possible reconstructions. So why would groups just starting out recreate where the Guard was ten years ago?" One such group which shall remain nameless – mainly because I can't remember their name, fielded three Centurions and about four legionaries. When asked why, they said they all wanted to be a Centurion! Some display that must have been. Another group's Centurion had totally in-accurate kit on and his reply to being asked why was "I'm the Centurion, I can wear what I like". Was it any wonder why we got annoyed when the public come up to us and said "We saw your lot up at <wherever> on Sunday" when we never even set foot there or they said "Your lot were on the telly the other night" when it was some tacky Hollywood reconstruction. I know, I'm sounding like a snob but if you're going to do something then do it right, especially if all the research has been done for you. Right time to get off the soap box and continue my journey through my legion-ary service.

I'll give you a run down of History in Action Kelmarsh as we've just been talking about it. I enjoyed Kelmarsh in the beginning apart from the final parade as already described. There were stalls selling all sorts of weird and wonderful produce, materials and ready made armour and weapons for re-enactors or the public to buy. A lot of what was on offer was just tat or "for display pur-poses only" that is, it'll look good on the mantlepiece. About a fortnight before the event a medieval village was built on site to be occupied by some of the merchants or re-enactors giving dem-onstrations. Obviously the buildings weren't made of permanent materials but they did look good and gave a great impression of what a medieval street might have looked like.

My wife, Sue came with me one time and because someone dropped out she ended up dressing in the ladies kit and looking after the shop. She enjoyed it although she found it tiring but had a great time in the beer tent on the first night the next day swear-ing never to touch rough cider again!

Susie and I at Kelmarsh

It was at that event that three spitfires flew over the site and did a bit of a display. We had finished our display and were back at our living history camp. The arena was in full swing with which ever group had followed us and the crowds were either watching or milling about. Suddenly there was the familiar roar of the Rolls Royce Merlin engine overhead and the spitfires started their aerial display. Everything stopped (apart from the group in the arena) to watch the display going on above them. It must have been disheartening for the arena group when your entire audience stop watching you and stare into the skies and how bizarre to have a battle with Vikings or whatever whilst spitfires flew overhead.

Sue had tears of pride as she watched these magnificent aircraft go through their paces and I must admit I had a lump in my throat too. Once the aerial acrobatics were over, everybody carried on with their previous exploits.

As usual we attended God's waiting room in the evenings and did the final parade at the end of the days. I did Kelmarsh a few more times but it was losing its appeal for me. As with all these events, they are there to make money and for a family the cost can be enormous.

The French had a similar history festival "La Histoire Festival Vivante" in a place called Marle in Northern France. As you know I have a liking for foreign trips so was one of the first to put my name down. Although the journeys are tiring and cramped in a minibus the trips themselves are usually very enjoyable and this was no exception. We returned to Marle a couple of years running and were very well looked after. One of the things from Marle that went down in Guard history was "The house of beer". The place where we displayed was on a archaeological park with reconstructed buildings. One such building contained a bar and a little hatch opened on the side and man passed a beer through to a Guard member, news of this facility travelled like wildfire through the men and a queue formed at the hatch. The beer was passed through to every man and it turned out that we were allowed to have free beer from this bar. On entering the building there was a rustic bar with enormous barrels and a man filling glasses and passing them to us either through the hatch or across the bar once we discovered that the house of beer was open.

We returned the following year on the understanding that "the house of beer" was still available, which of course it was. It was on the first trip to Marle that I had my first taste of the dessert panacotta. Before this time cheesecake was my favourite dessert and if it was on the menu then cheesecake it was. But once I'd had panacotta, my allegiance changed and that then became my dessert of choice.

On my first trip to this festival I, along with the rest of the Guard were involved in "The Battle of Marle". This took place near to our encampment as we came off the display field. The area around our camp had a reconstructed rampart and ditch and the other periods – I'm not sure who, maybe Vikings or that ilk, decided that they would prevent us from entering our living history camp. Chris sent half of us to the end of the rampart where we could go into the camp area, the rest would enter via the proper entrance after challenging the "enemy". They were blocking the way waving their swords and axes completely unaware of the sec-

ond group of Romans marching up on their rear. Once they'd realised that we'd split into two groups and had hemmed them in the
battle commenced. We pushed with our shields as did they and
the resulting crush was quite amusing. I pushed into the enemy
with my shield trying to force them back. Denis Evans was to my
left and was doing the same but unfortunately he was on the edge
of the ditch and lost his footing. I looked over my shoulder to
see him disappearing into the ditch with a look of horror on his
face, suddenly from behind me Seggy (Anthony Segalini) also lost
his footing and fell into the ditch on top of Denis. I continued to
push and we gained the upperhand, a couple of the enemy were
being pushed over some pallisade stakes. Luckily they managed
to avoid the sharp ends – just. It could have had dire consequences
if one or more had been skewered on them. The battle was won
by the Guard and we gained new respect from the other groups.
Denis had a few bruises as did Seggy but they survived with just
the bruises and some dents in their armour.

Feeding the troops, Marle, France

My last time in Marle in twenty fifteen coincided with a protest against French cutbacks to the culture budget. During the course of a ceremony to present Chris with a specially commissioned vine stick, it was requested that everyone on the field, therefore all the re-enactors, should lie facedown on the ground for a length of time. This was to signify the death of culture or something like that. We never really got told the exact meaning of what and why we did it but I'm sure it had some historical significance and will turn up in a book or something sometime in the future!

15

Going back a few years to nineteen ninety three, I got a call from Chris. The Post Office were promoting a set of stamps based on some finds from the collections at Caerleon museum. They wanted Roman Soldiers so it was myself, Chris Haines and John Burdon that provided the backdrop for the stamps. We got into kit and the photographer clicked away to the artistic director's directions. We held a giant postage stamp in all sorts of positions outside the main museum building. Then once they'd got the pics they wanted with the giant stamp, the artistic director thought it would be good to have a picture with a real postage stamp stuck on my nose. I went along with it as you do but the picture was used on the front page of a local paper, The Newport Free Press, which meant that every house in Newport and the surrounding area would get a copy. The picture would have been great had it not been for the postage stamp.

● Stamp of approval: Roman Legionnaire Fred Stacey of Caerleon Road, Newport, displays one of the new set of Royal Mail stamps, launched at the Legionary Museum in Caerleon last week. **Fred's a first class soldier!**

I had lots of comments about it with people handing me copies of the paper ("In case I missed it") as if I would. The one thing about doing these extra promos and the main displays is we don't know when or where they will be used. I'd try to find out from the people organising the gig but quite often they weren't sure (or they are playing their cards close to their chest, so to speak).

You will notice that a lot of what we did apart from the displays involved the museum at Caerleon. We had a very close working relationship with the staff there and at the National Museum in Cardiff, of which the Caerleon museum is a subsidiary and it was the ideal location for these minor promotional events. As I live in South Wales and not too far from the museum I got asked to do a lot of the promos and events there. I didn't mind doing these things and as you probably guessed, I quite enjoyed doing them especially if they were to be on the telly or in the papers. Susie says I am a narcissistic devil and she is absolutely right. Probably.

16

In 2010 we were asked to take part in the iconic British TV series Dr.Who. A few members including myself headed for Margam Park near Port Talbot in South Wales to help set up a Roman encampment ready for filming. Naturally the ground was boggy and the previous week had been covered in a layer of snow. It turned out the program makers had done a recce in the snow so had no idea what the ground was actually like. Several attempts to get the tent pegs to stay in the ground we decided to go to the pub for lunch. On return we eventually got the whole thing sorted ready for the action to take place. Between the tents large areas were marked with tape. This was to allow the special effects people to create a complete legionary encampment with CGI which in the final program looked half decent.

On the morning of filming we arrived at the production village and were told to get into kit, head for make up (clearly a bit of fake mud on our legs and faces makes us look more Roman) then get some breakfast. It was another one those hurry up and wait situations. After a lot of hanging about the call came to be on set. A small coach was sent to take us there but Chris after a bit of discussion decided we'd march over to the filming area. I'm glad we did it as it gave us a bit of kudos with crew and the professional extras. To get to the actual set we had negotiate a boggy slope that was really awkward to climb in kit.

The filming was the usual stop start affair with lots of hanging about in the cold. Standing around on cold ground whilst wearing sandals does not make for a comfortable experience. The special effects people had braziers in strategic places as part of the set, they were gas powered so when the director called action they burst into life. When they called cut they were, unfortunately, turned off again, if only they left just one turned on so we could warm our feet. We did find that they had a small fire around the back which we made full use of.

I would have liked to have had a photo of me exiting the Tardis in full armour but we were told no phones or cameras on set. It turned out that some of the professional luvvies had their phones with them anyway. The Tardis comes as a flat pack affair with a single bulb on the inside, quite disappointing really but at least I can say I've been inside the real tardis!

An interesting tactic the film people used on this was to have a group march up and down this narrow track and to have a few wander around. I was one of the wanderers. After doing this for a while they called cut and said that tea and biscuits were being served up this slight incline away from the encampment. When I got to see the program, I could see why they had us wandering up and down and why they called us for tea. The wandering was repeated and cloned to make it look busy from a distance and when they called tea they continued filming as we made our way up the slope towards the camera. On the finished composite image I can identify myself in at least four places. There was a bit of night filming which involved myself and John Hindle (Madge) having a small scene with the character River Song played by Alex Kingston. I got to stare into Alex Kingston's eyes over a couple of takes.

Prior to this I had a minor "stunt" to perform, which involved running across the path of an approaching horse ridden by a professional stunt woman. I was never in danger as I was quite away from the horse, but with fancy camerawork, namely compressed perspective, I looked closer than I was. The stunt woman was dressed in the similar clothes as Alex and she galloped into the scene as I run across in front of her. She jumps off the horse to be replaced by Alex and runs to where Madge and I block her way (this is where I get to stare into her eyes). Chris Jones (Petshop) was volunteered to hold the horse as he owned a petshop so was best qualified to deal with animals. From small pets to horse wrangler in a day. Once this was done we were released from filming as the crew set up for more night time filming on a reconstructed Stonehenge on the top of a hill above where we were filming. This was dubbed Foamhenge. It was cold and tiring but great fun and I still "dine out" on the fact that I was in Dr Who. Incidentally the Dr in these episodes was played by Matt Smith who when we finished thanked us, unusual for luvvies even to acknowledge we exist.

17

In the early two thousands we had a trip to Spain to a place ninety or so kilometres South of Barcelona. Tarragona is an area rich in Roman remains with aqueducts, amphitheatre and other left overs from Imperial Rome. We were to perform at a public park called the Camp de Mart, so the long trek took place to get us there. I can't remember much about the journeys, whether we flew or went by road I don't know (the problem with age and so many and varied journey's in the Guard, I think we went overland). Tarragona was one of the nicer foreign jobs with fine weather (actually it was extremely hot). The displays were very well attended and our numbers were swelled by the The Gemina Project from the Netherlands. We (The Guard) did a few minor displays on an outdoor stage for some local schools.

On stage at the Camp de Mart, Tarragona, Spain

These displays went well with the kids lapping it up. Chris in his infinite wisdom decided that during the charge we'd leap from the stage and continue the charge into the tiered seating at the kids. It went down a storm on the first display with kids and the adults in uproar. On the second display we leapt from the stage which was about four feet high to charge the audience only this time I overbalanced backwards and fell onto my back with my legs in the air. The kids were in fits of laughter at this, luckily I had briefs on but I still think I completed a part of their education. The displays went well with thousands of spectators who very much enjoyed the spectacle especially when blood was spilled. During exercitus (exercises or battle training), Rob Ingram took a hit on the nose causing a lot of blood to stream down the front of his armour. That armour still has traces as it was difficult to remove. As with quite a few events abroad the organisers like to add a bit of something by having a big march with the Romans at the front. This being Spain was no different except they decided that the Pompa as they called it was to be headed by a bull. We were to march from the old city to the Camp De Mart with a handler leading the bull on a rope. First we had to march up the hill to the old city where the bull was waiting to lead us. As we marched up the hill which was arduous we came to a buttress on the city wall and behind this the bull with his handler was waiting.

The bull took one look at us and took off in the opposite direction dragging the handler behind him. We continued on up the hill and was brought to a halt while we waited for the bull to return. After a while the handler reappeared with said bull and we were told to stay absolutely still, which we did, we weren't daft!. So we stood so the bull could see us and hopefully get used to all these men stood around in bright shiny metal suits. A couple of the boys were told to walk slowly towards the animal to make him get used to us some more. They were encouraged to stroke him which they did rather nervously. Then we had to gently shake our armour plates and jingle our cingulum (apron attached to our belt) to get him used to the noise. Eventually it was decided that the bull would be OK so we were lined up either side of the path as Mr Bully was brought through. I was stood opposite Martin as we waited for him to pass. He had just started to pass us by when he decided he was having none of it and went beserk. From over Martin's side I heard what could only be described as a shrake sound as the bull's horns scraped across the mail on Martin's chest. As I was about four feet away from the animal I wasn't going to wait for my turn on the horns. I threw my shield and pila to the ground and climbed the wall behind me rather quickly. I wasn't going to be impaled on those horns. Eventually they managed to get a handle on the animal and we marched down the hill with the bull fighting it all the way.

Later on, I noticed a lot of bruises on the top of my arms where the armour dug in as I scrambled up the wall. Better that than a hole in my gut.

18

I have spoken before about the hard core of regular members and how there was an outer core of members who dip in and stay for a while then leave for whatever reason. I was for a while the only member in Wales. Since then there had been a couple more members to the Welsh contingent in the form of school teacher Steve Hayes and pet shop owner Chris Jones. Geraint Llewellyn was with us for a while and when we were all together we were known as the Taffia. Geraint left to pursue a career in weight / power-lifting. Apart from Caerleon with its amphitheatre we rarely got to do jobs anywhere else in Wales. We did a small promo at Dolacothi Gold Mine in mid Wales which made a minor news item. In two thousand and nine the Guard were asked to take part in a promo for the Six Nations rugby tournament. Filming would take place in December (naturally) in the Brecon Beacons. Filming is always in the winter for some reason, I suppose if I'd been a civil war re-enactor with all the heavy clothing involved, filming would take place in the summer!

Very early one snowy morning we were to meet at a village hall near Merthyr Tydfil that would be used as base camp for the filming. This was where we would be changing once ready we were then taken by minibus to the filming area. There was a layer of snow on the ground and initially it wasn't too cold but this was to change as the day wore on. The place where filming took place was a couple of miles away from base camp next to a reservoir with the mountain Pen y Fan in the near distance. We had to walk from a parking area over a gateway, then a fast flowing stream and on to the place where the BBC determined was where they wanted to film. Although there were dry and reasonably flat areas, they decided on the boggiest bit of ground for us to march up and down. We (the Guard) did what we were told as usual with the minimum of fuss whereas the "actors" insisted on wearing wellington boots because their feet were getting cold and wet.

We may have been a bunch of oldies but we were certainly tough nuts to crack. Filming started late because of the logistics of moving everyone to the set. Once everyone was in place we did the take which of course required us to march through boggy ground, not once, but several times to get different angles. There was lots of hanging around as always.

I took a small video camera with me to the set and got one of the crew to gets some shots. With extra footage taken by me in breaks etc. I managed to make a reasonable "Making of" documentary. This is available to view on Youtube. As the filming day went on it began to snow more and more but the BBC film people didn't mind because they had their big boots and parkas, we were only the talent so it didn't matter!

After marching up and down a few times we took a break while they brought in a drone camera. This was the first time I'd seen anything like this and thought to myself "I want one". As it turned out about a year later everybody had one and they were so widely available they were cropping up everywhere. Unfortunately these drones as they became called had acquired a bad reputation so I was reluctant to get one.

Anyway, once the drone had been set up we were marched up and down again while the camera flew around us.

Then it was the turn of the Celts to do their bit. Chris Jones a relatively new member at the time, organised members of a local rugby club to play the part of the Celts. Initially it was exciting being involved in filming, but after several takes in heavy snow without any shelter or warm drinks things started to become arduous. Eventually the Romans of which I was one were sent back to the production base for lunch, while the Celts did some shots.

We were being fed at a local pub which caused a bit of excitement amongst the locals as a bunch of Romans filed into the pub restaurant. We warmed ourselves by the fire and imbibed some ale whilst watching daytime telly until we had to board the minibus back to the set. When we got back it transpired that the Celts were still at the site and the production people were expecting them to stay there and carry on filming. They hadn't had a break for five hours and were becoming mutinous. The snow started to come down heavier and as we were out on the Brecon Beacons there was a real possibility that we could be trapped. I wouldn't have minded if it meant a free ride in a rescue helicopter!

Eventually the production crew realised the gravity of the situation and quickly got the final shots and called a wrap.

Myself and Geraint with some of the crew

The final promo was one of a series and the one with the Romans was the best, you can find it on YouTube if you need proof!!

19

As I have said before, one of my personal highlights of being in the Guard was the yearly trip to foreign shores. One of the best trips in later years of my Guard membership was to a place in Germany called Xanten. Here they have an archaeological park (APX) spread over several acres with reconstructed villas and the like. In the mid 2000's they completed and opened the main museum housing some of the most amazing finds from the park and elsewhere. On a previous trip we were given a guided tour of the museum during construction. Part of the museum is built over Roman ruins which allows the visitor to see how the buildings were.

Xanten, Germany. I'm wearing the black bearskin

The event in Xanten is always well attended by the public and Roman re-enactors from all over Europe. The first time we went it was nice, warm and sunny during the first display. Then came the Pompa which took place in the reconstructed amphitheatre. The ground inside the amphitheatre is covered in deep rough sand with little bits of shell in it, thus making it murder to march on in sandals. Anyway, everybody marched in and around the arena which, despite the sand under our feet was good as it gave you a sense of what it must have been like back in the day. The crowds cheered as all the Roman groups marched around the outer edge of the arena headed by the Guard. Once everybody was in their correct positions, an altar was brought into the centre ready for a libation. The priests started the chanting and speeches were made in Latin. As the libation was poured onto the altar it started clouding over and suddenly the heavens opened right on cue with the heaviest rain I'd ever seen. This was followed by a massive thunderstorm right overhead and as you can imagine, made everyone wearing armour and carrying long sticks with metal on top very nervous. Chris gave the order to march off and once we were under the arches at the entrance stopped us so that we were in shelter. The thunderstorm was in full swing with extremely bright flashes and very loud bangs. I love thunderstorms but this was something else, you could feel the charge in the air. It was the turn of the second contubernium to go for their lunch break so Madge (John Hindle) decided to march us back to the changing area where we could have a cuppa and food. As we marched along with Madge calling the step "sin dex sin dex" there was a massive flash right by us and the loudest bang ever. The storm was right overhead. This was followed by a few screams from nearby. The rain fell in massive drops and we were continuing to plod back to base when there was another big flash and a few more screams. Madge continued calling the step when I took the executive decision and shouted "Fuck the step, run!" so we ran the rest of the way.

It turned out that when we heard the screams, somebody had been struck by the lightning. All hell broke loose as there were sirens coming from all directions with fire trucks, ambulances and police entering the park. Three air ambulances flew into the arena as well and the event was called off. The German government took the decision to stop the event as more storms were headed in that direction. When we went back to the same spot later there was a hole in the ground where the lightning struck. Such is the power of nature.

So we had a choice, head back home or stay the three days as intended. The organisers didn't mind what we did as the accommodation was booked anyway. We opted to stay, I mean, a free mini break in Germany, no contest.

Myself, Madge and Geraint decided one afternoon to take a wander into Xanten town possibly to look for presents to bring home. Geraint needed to change some money or needed change for something or other, can't remember what, so we decided to go into a bar and have one drink and carry on. So we ordered some beers and an old gent got chatting to us and bought us all a drink. We then bought him one and during the course of the conversation he mentioned something about a festival taking place in the next village, he'd take us there if we were interested.

As we had time and it was our last day in Xanten we thought why not. The old gent said he had to go somewhere along the way and told us to walk through this field and that he'd meet us at the other side. We made jokes with ourselves that he was having a laugh at our expense and that we would be walking for miles and then have to come back. There were a lot of strawberries and blackberries along the route so we had something to munch on our journey. As we came out at the other end of the field, there true to his word was the old gent. We had walked straight to the next village and sure enough there was something going on. People lined the streets and a police car with lights flashing slowly came around the corner. This was followed by a procession of German males with rifles over their shoulders marching along. At the head of the column were several flag bearers carrying large flags with emblems on them. They must have represented the villages or groups to which they belonged.

A band marched behind them playing German oompah music. As the back end of the procession passed us we tagged on at the back and followed them to their destination. The flags had designs that we couldn't make out and at one point we did question whether we should be marching behind them. It was of course, totally innocent and was a festival or something to do with local shooting clubs, hence the rifles. After the march, the band, flag bearers and the men with rifles marched into a field and the public gathered around the edge to watch the proceedings. There was a lot of flag waving to the sound of the band and then some speeches and presentations and then they all marched out of the field and disbanded. After that they all went to the festival site which included a very large marquee. Once inside we were made very welcome and then the bands marched in and played a set of German marching tunes on the dance floor which was very good.

We bought a few drinks then as time went on we got talking to the locals who started buying us drinks so after several we became quite merry shall we say. The oompah band finished their set and there was then a break while food was served. I can't remember what or if we had any – we must have had something but I can't remember. The evening entertainment started with a pop band playing covers and there were a lot of posh frocks on the dance floor. We decided to throw some shapes so got up and danced too, to the amusement or disdain of the locals. We were invited to join some people on their table and more drinks were consumed. Very late on in the evening we were at the bar drinking with a small group including the mayor of one of the villages / towns and a gentleman in the grey uniform jacket of the Third Reich (old habits die hard I suppose). When it was time to go they even gave us a lift back to Xanten and the archaeological park where we were staying. What I didn't mention was this took place the day/ night before we were to journey to the ferry home so we had to be up early. I don't know what time we left the party or what time we got back, I was a little bit smashed. It seemed like I'd only just got into bed when the door burst open and Graeme Walker came in shouting at the top of his voice to get up. I felt like nothing on earth but I packed my things and got on the minibus and plonked myself into a seat and fell asleep. I slept as we drove out of Xanten until we stopped at a service station. I had some food and water then promptly went back to sleep. When we reached the next service stop I was feeling so much better. I am glad we went with the old gent to that festival, it was an experience that I will remember for a long time.

A very welcome beer, Xanten, Germany

The following year or two we went back to Xanten and just as before it rained heavily and after one display, the event was called off. We didn't stay the full time and packed up and left early. You win some, you lose some.

In 2011 we made a trip to Germany again but this time it was to Trier. Here we were to perform our usual displays with the other groups from the continent joining us. Trier has some fantastic ruins from the Roman period, one of the most spectacular being the Porta Nigre, The Black Gate.

It was from this point that we would start our displays, we marched from here, through the town and into the display arena. It was quite a gruelling march, but quite enjoyable which for me was unusual as long marches were not always my favourite (I think a warm climate helps a great deal). Close to the display area were underground tunnels and there was a sort of play going on that moved through tunnels and in some places live diaramas took place. It was all very fanciful and nobody was entirely sure what the story was about. With the lighting and the sound it was quite interesting and as I had a small video camera I recorded it several times from different angles and edited it into something coherent-ish with music added by me. It was OK and gives a good representation of the event. I filmed the Guard setting up camp and packing it all away again once we had finished. At the time of writing, I still have yet to put this footage together. I filmed the Guard getting ready and setting off on the journey to Trier and will put this together at some point although I did edit a "part one" of Petshop, mine and Geraint's journey in Petshop's van.

On one occasion whilst touring through the tunnels with Geraint, Ben Jeal, Petshop and others one of the diorama areas was unoccupied. Geraint decided he would go inside and mock a scene. I recorded this and with a bit of editing it turned out very funny and amusing. At the time, as we had all gathered to watch, members of the public also gathered with us and were really taken in. On the video you can hear someone saying "Oh wooow" Some of the evenings we would go into town for a bite to eat and drink. At one bar they had an old gramaphone playing old dance music outside in the town square. Couples would get up and waltz in the street outside the bar. It was quite atmospheric and reminiscent of a time gone by.

I have to say, the German trips had always been enjoyable and we were looked after quite well. The German people were very hospitable and enthusiastic about what we were doing which goes a long way when you're on the field, audience appreciation makes it worthwhile.

20

I was always quite fit and looking at photographs of me in the earlier years I was quite lean too. I did put on a bit of weight and found that the lorica segmentata was a bit tight in places. I also found that I was not feeling up to standard at some displays.

In 2012 the Guard was forty years old and was to recreate the original march from Bentham village hall to Witcombe Roman Villa. The Guard was formed in 1972 as part of a pageant to raise funds for the building of the hall so as part of the fortieth anniversary the march was to be undertaken again. I was looking forward to it even though it was a long march and at this time I was the Guards Vexillarius – the flag carrier so would be marching at the front. It went well but as we were getting closer to the Villa I began to feel quite ill. With encouragement from the boys I managed to struggle on and get to the end. I really felt unwell and just sat quietly as fresh apple juice was given to us. I eventually I began to feel better but but didn't know what caused the feeling.

Susie and I had an allotment at that time and we went one day to do some work there. We arrived unpacked the tools and I felt ill again, feeling really weak. We made a cup of tea and I began to feel better. I went to the doctor's because I was getting severe spasms in my gullet so blood tests were performed. It turned out that I was diabetic. Suddenly everything fell into place. The times I'd felt unwell during Guard jobs and other times wasn't down to drink, I was just slipping towards a coma! (so dramatic). I carried on for a short while but eventually made the decision to leave the Guard after I'd completed twenty-five years. It was a difficult decision but with long periods without food, the heat and fluid loss from wearing the armour and the possibility of having to take medication was too much to mess with. I decided that I would stay as an associate member and do things for the Guard such as take photos and create videos. My tenure in the Guard was an incredible time going places that I'd never dreamt of going and meeting people such as Royalty that I'd never dream of meeting. Taking part in TV programs, some of them iconic such as Dr Who, and events that due to cutbacks may never happen again. One event I am really proud of is meeting the famous film director Ken Russell (he directed Tommy and Women in Love) and taking part in his last film before his death. I asked if I could have a photo with him and he gladly obliged standing on the green screen with myself, Chris, Mike and Geraint. It is one of my favourite photos of my Guard career. This is a prime example of doing things through the Guard that I might never had done otherwise.

Ken Russell with a few members.

The Guard, at the time of writing, is approaching it's fiftieth year and with Chris approaching and Mike in his eighties I wonder how much longer it will carry on. I am proud to have been a member, to have taken part in some spectacular events among other things, it has given me fond memories and lifelong friendships.

Printed in Great Britain
by Amazon